THE
RESOURCEFUL
RENOVATOR

RESO
RE

THE RESOURCEFUL RENOVATOR

A Gallery of Ideas for Reusing Building Materials

Jennifer Corson, M. Arch.

CHELSEA GREEN PUBLISHING COMPANY
White River Junction, Vermont
Totnes, England

This book is dedicated to my mother, Moreen,
who could always see the possibilities
well before any seed was planted.

Designed by Jill Shaffer.
Edited by Einar Christensen, P. Eng.

Printed in Canada.
First printing, October 2000
03 02 01 00   1 2 3 4 5

Library of Congress Cataloging-in-Publication Data
Corson, Jennifer, 1967-
     The resourceful renovator : a gallery of ideas for reusing building
          materials / Jennifer Corson.
          p.   cm.
     Includes bibliographical references and index.
     ISBN 1-890132-51-9 (alk. paper)
     1. Buildings—Salvaging. 2. Building materials—Recycling.
          3. Construction and demolition debris—Recycling. I. Title.

TH449 .C67 2000
691—dc21   00-043106

Chelsea Green Publishing Company
P.O. Box 428
White River Junction, VT 05001
www.chelseagreen.com

THE REAL GOODS SOLAR LIVING BOOKS

Real Goods Trading Company in Ukiah, California, was founded in 1978 to make available new tools to help people live self-sufficiently and sustainably. Through seasonal catalogs, a periodical (*The Real Goods News*), a bi-annual *Solar Living Sourcebook*, as well as retail outlets and a Web site (www.realgoods.com), Real Goods provides a broad range of tools for independent living.

"Knowledge is our most important product" is the Real Goods motto. To further its mission, Real Goods has joined with Chelsea Green Publishing Company to co-create and co-publish the Real Goods Solar Living Book series. The titles in this series are written by pioneering individuals who have firsthand experience in using innovative technology to live lightly on the planet. Chelsea Green books are both practical and inspirational, and they enlarge our view of what is possible as we enter the new millennium.

Stephen Morris
President, Chelsea Green

John Schaeffer
President, Real Goods

CONTENTS

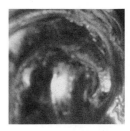

TABLES AND CHARTS

CONVERSION TABLE

LINEAR MEASURE

1 centimeter	=	0.39 inches
1 inch	=	2.54 centimeters
1 foot	=	30.48 centimeters
1 meter	=	39.37 inches
1 meter	=	1.09 yards
1 cubic meter (m³)	=	1.31 cubic yards
1 yard	=	0.9144 meter
1 kilometer	=	0.62137 mile
1 mile	=	1.6094 kilometers
1 board foot	=	1 lineal foot of 1 x 12-inch board
board feet	=	(length x thickness x width) ÷ 12
		(e.g., one 8-foot-long 2 x 4 = 5⅓ board feet)

WEIGHT

1 kilogram	=	2.2 pounds
1 pound	=	0.45 kilogram
1 ton (U.S.)	=	2,200 pounds
1 tonne (metric)	=	2,204.6 pounds

MONETARY (APPROXIMATE VALUE JULY, 2000)

1 dollar (U.S.)	=	1.50 dollar (CAD)
1 dollar (CAD)	=	0.69 (U.S.)

OTHER USEFUL CONVERSIONS

To find the diameter of a circle, multiply the circumference by 0.31831.

To find the circumference of a circle, multiply the diameter by 3.1416.

To find the area of a circle, multiply the square of diameter by 0.7854.

Dry wood averages about 3 pounds per board foot.

PREFACE

We must be the change we wish to see in the world.

—Mahatma Gandhi

For the past ten years I have been trying successfully to design and build with less. By "less," I mean less materials, less money, less clutter, less impact on the environment, less complication . . . just "less." The "more" has often detoured this approach in a variety of ways. Clients have more available bank credit, more land, more gadgets to store, more desires for out-of-scale grandeur, more magazines to look at, more options available . . . "more." Added to this are, more available high-tech fixes, more research literature, more marketing from product manufacturers, and more desperate environmental concerns to make one react.

My initial interest in writing this book was sparked while I was working on my architectural thesis in Guinea, West Africa, in 1990. Elders, and indeed most of the community in the small village of Timbi-Medina, in the interior of Guinea, had always lived in the

A *caz,* the traditional mud building of Guinea, West Africa.

caz, a traditional round mud building. These beautiful structures had thatched roofs and were always the most comfortable buildings to sleep in. During the day, the heavy earth walls with the over-hanging roof kept out the midday heat, and cool evenings were moderated as the walls released some of the warmth stored during the day. But modern housing influences from the capital city of Conakry and farther afield had begun to push for uniform construction of houses with modular brick and concrete block. Concrete block and fired brick were considered "rich" person's materials—"rich" having something to do with being able to afford a modern material, whether this material was suited to the region or not. Not only was fired brick beyond the budget of most people, but I soon learned that farmers were losing their once-fertile farming soil to drought and erosion. It wasn't just the climate; many adjacent regions were not encountering this same difficulty. The soil quality was deteriorating because the trees were being cut down for firewood. Some of the firewood was being used for cooking, but most was burned to fire clay bricks for the many new houses being built for the residents of the village.

A French agricultural aid agency, trying to combat the loss the trees and fertile soil, proposed that the community build their new homes from a different type of brick, one that didn't require cutting down trees for firing brick. Air-dried earth brick has been used for centuries throughout the world. One Timbi-Medina homeowner consented to have his family's new home built from this material. The locals teased the man for wasting his money on another earthen building, no better than the one he grew up in. After only the first ten courses of brick had been erected, many other villagers asked the local contractor to build their new homes from this

Outdoor brick kiln in Guinea.

Air-dried earth brick home in Timbi-Medina, Guinea.

same material. The new home was a beautiful, warm, golden color, containing arches and doorways that reflected the work of talented masons, reviving a skilled trade in the community. The air-dried brick was cheaper than either concrete or fired brick and the construction much more efficient, because all of the earth came from a pit within a few yards of the new home. This tiny community inspired the construction of many new schools and public buildings in Guinea out of this same material. Now the trees stand proudly, and the farmers can reap the harvest. This experience helped me to see how our choices of building materials directly affect whole ecosystems.

Sitting down to write this book was a test in many ways. I not only had the challenge of gathering my thoughts and experiences and putting them forward in a cohesive manner (not an easy task for a rambling gal), but I had to start by building a desk on which to write. I looked at the old doors at our used building material store, the Renovators Resource, and found three possible options that would serve to rest on two used filing cabinets. The first door was priced at $30, and would require two cuts to fit within a designated place in the room. The second was less expensive, but would be two inches short in one direction—not a great "shortcoming." The third door was perfect. It was the least expensive and would fit perfectly with no cuts required. I'm off to a good start . . . affordably reusing primary building materials.

ACKNOWLEDGMENTS

MY BUSINESS PARTNER, Susan Helliwell, and the team at the Renovators Resource Inc. in Halifax, Nova Scotia, are a persevering crew. Every day they carefully save what so many others are quick to throw out. Many of the stories and examples used in the book are from firsthand experience at Renovators. As well, Pick & Shovel's "Resourceful Renovator" crew and partners Johanna Eliot and Michael MacDonald worked together to produce a great television series. Some of the show's best episodes are featured in this book. All of these people complete the circle, and make up for what's missed. Without them, I would still be trying to build earth houses in soggy climates.

The talent of the team who worked together on this book is astounding. Photographer Kelly Bentham knows what shots to take and how to take them. Only he would climb into tiny spaces on Sunday mornings to get the perfect shot. The "hatch man," and my love, Keith Robertson, has such a way with an ink pen and weak instructions that he turned disjointed requests into solid representations, as seen throughout the book. Engineer and editor Einar Christensen is the most supportive person I know. His expertise on "waste" and "recycling" was invaluable throughout the editing process. He made it possible to send 40,000 words to the publisher without fear of refusal. Thanks team!

I'd like to thank the following people and organizations for their interest, support, and contributions to this project: Barrett Lumber Company, Robbie Bays (Oakdene Centre), Lorin Brehaut, Helen Brown, Dan Chassie, Louis and Pamela Collins, Daltech Faculty of Architecture, Scott Fotheringham, Rita and Arwed Gerstenberger (Nova Tile and Marble), Emmanuel Jannasch, Miller Demolition, James Nicholson, Nova Scotia Department of Natural Resources, Pittsburgh Plate Glass Company, Gordon Plume, Chris Reardon, Norbert Senf, Sherry Schalm (Tangerine Tileworks), Sandra Strain, Margo Thompson (NAHB Research Center), Peter Tomlin, Paul Webb, Joyce Wisdom (ReUse Center), and Hilary Writer.

THE
RESOURCEFUL
RENOVATOR

INTROD

UCTION

A definition of how to achieve "shelter": Economy + Beauty + Durability = Time

—Shelter, 1973

Humans began to build their shelters four hundred thousand years ago. Early dwellings were made of mud, grass, sticks, animal hides—anything that could be found at hand. These early inhabitants also discovered fire, probably by accident. Over the thousands of years since then, we have learned to manipulate fire to manufacture and shape metal parts, tools, and implements, ceramic tiles, panes of glass, pallets of brick, cut stone, and wood products—the basic building materials.

Lost opportunity to reclaim material.

"Fire" is a metaphor for energy. Ever since we moved out of caves and began to construct our own shelter, our buildings and furnishings have required the input of energy. Some of that energy is in the form of human and animal labor. All energy might be said to originate from the Sun; we have used the Sun's energy directly to dry bricks or lumber, and less directly through the use of water and wind to power machinery. And since the Industrial Revolution, we have consumed vast quantities of solar energy stored as fossil fuels—the remains of ancient animals once powered by carbohydrates that ancient green plants produced by photosynthesis.

When we begin to understand where a building material originates, how it is extracted from nature, and how much energy is embodied in the process of changing a raw resource into a useful product,

then we can start to comprehend the global impact of our use of that resource. And when we know how much value—in the form of many different kinds of energy and ingenuity and plain hard work—has already been added to transform ore or earth or tree into radiators or doorknobs or tongue-and-groove flooring, we will be very reluctant to simply throw away such valuable items. And nothing ever really goes "away."

That is why it is necessary to include the costs of conservation and recycling—so-called embedded or embodied costs—in a construction or renovation project. The fact is that all of us pay for garbage services, landfill operations, and for the loss of our natural resources. It won't be long until we run out of some of these resources, or can't afford to mine or harvest them any longer. We already pay for the pollution created by the extraction, transportation, and processing of materials—in the cost of health care, water and air treatment, dying forests, and depleted fish stocks. If we

---

PRINCIPLES FOR SUSTAINABLE DESIGN AND BUILDING

One of the most knowledgeable sources for information on recycled building materials is the Center for Resourceful Building Technology (CRBT) in Missoula, Montana. For eight years, CRBT has educated builders, renovators, designers, and the public on issues related to housing and the environment, with an emphasis on building materials and technologies that place less strain on regional and global ecosystems. The Center follows this set of principles for more sustainable designing and building:

1. **Make efficient use of limited natural resources by:**

   - preserving the resources, energy, and labor invested in a product through longevity in application or potential for reuse;

   - extending the resource base by using less material to achieve the same or better performance than other materials;

   - substituting a more-abundant for a less-abundant resource, a renewable for a nonrenewable material, or a recyclable for a nonrecyclable material;

   - reducing cumulative environmental impacts of resource consumption by limiting air pollution, which affects climate change; water pollution, which leads to watershed damage; and habitat loss and loss of biodiversity.

2. **Demonstrate recyclability or renewability by choosing products that are:**

   - made of reused or recycled components;

   - biodegradable, or readily recyclable through existing technologies and collection programs;

   - recoverable for recycling or reuse from their applied state.

3. **Reduce energy use of buildings by:**

   - requiring comparatively low total lifetime energy inputs, including energy from extraction and related land and water reclamation, processing and related pollution abatement, transportation, installation, lifetime maintenance, and material recovery and recycling;

   - utilizing a high proportion of lifetime energy inputs from renewable sources;

   - reducing the amount of operating energy a building will require.

think of building products as "locked-up energy"; if we realize that for every item salvaged, virgin resources can be left in place; if every person building, renovating, or repairing practiced the concept of conserving embodied energy, then a substantial amount of energy would be preserved for when we really need it. I have begun each chapter in this book with a description of the origin and manufacturing history of each of six basic building materials—wood, metal, stone, brick, glass, and ceramic—to help show just how expensive, and valuable, they are.

Many North American structures have reached an age when they must either be removed or completely refurbished. Building owners, contractors, and developers once believed that the only solution was demolition, but progressive thinkers now recognize the possibilities for reusing and recycling construction materials. The traditional method of demolishing a building is to use an excavator or wrecking ball to knock it down into a rubble pile and then cart the debris away to the landfill. In some regions where tipping fees are exorbitant, waste is shipped hundreds of miles to areas with lower tipping fees. This extra transport may save tipping dollars, but requires additional fuel and produces more emissions than necessary. Thankfully, pressure from many sides has begun to change this practice. The rising costs, and even bans at landfills, will motivate contractors to separate demolition debris, paying the higher disposal fees only for the material that cannot be recycled. Perhaps the heavy cost of getting rid of nonrecyclable waste will also inspire builders and those in industries that manufacture building products to consider total lifetime energy inputs when designing and selecting new materials and products.

Once the decision has been made to demolish a building, and all of the reusable items, including plumbing and lighting fixtures, interior fittings, windows, and appliances, have been removed, the remaining materials, consisting mostly of wood, drywall, concrete, metal, masonry, glass, and roofing materials, ought to be recycled whenever possible. Extra effort is required to separate the materials on the demolition site, but extra benefits are gained by doing so, as noted in the following chart. As an example, a load of concrete block, stone, or brick, delivered to a C&D recycler, can cost as little as $5 per ton for disposal. A mixed load of C&D material (containing some stone aggregate with other construction materials) can cost up to $200 per ton in some regions. The incentive for the contractor and homeowner to separate materials prior to disposal is clear.

The resourceful renovator can find many ways to participate in the new world of C&D recycling. The flow chart on page 6 is

FACT:

Less than 20 percent of the world's population consumes more than 80 percent of the world's resources. The average person living in: North America consumes 11.0 kilowatt-hours per hour; Germany consumes 6.0 kilowatt-hours per hour; China consumes 0.8 kilowatt-hours per hour.

—Dr. Hans-Peter Duerr, Max-Planck-Institut fuer Physik, Munich

VALUE OF SALVAGEABLE BUILDING MATERIALS AND THE COSTS TO REPLACE THEM

The values shown in the following chart are representative of the comparative cost between reuse and recycling, and buying new materials compared to used materials. Obvious savings can be gained both by salvaging and reselling building materials, and by buying used items.

BUILDING MATERIAL	PAID SALVAGE VALUE	PAID (OR CHARGED) TO RECYCLE MATERIAL +/-	NEW MATERIAL PURCHASE PRICE	USED MATERIAL PURCHASE PRICE	DENSITY OF MATERIAL
WOOD	$/lb.[1]	$/lb.[2]	$/bd. ft.[3]	$/bd. ft.[1]	lbs/bd.ft.[10]
Oak	0.35[a]	(0.02)	5.30–6.60	4.00	3.8–3.9
Maple	0.34[b]	(0.02)	3.60–12.00	3.30	2.9–3.7
Birch	0.30[b]	(0.02)	4.80–7.20	3.30	3.3–3.8
Ash	0.35[b]	(0.02)	4.80	n/a	2.8–3.5
Pine	0.31[c]	(0.02)	2.40–5.20	2.00	2.1–2.3
Spruce	0.28[c]	(0.02)	2.00	1.50	2.3
METAL	$/lb.[1]	$/lb.[4]	$/lb.[5]	$/lb.[8]	lbs./cu.ft.[10]
Aluminum	depends	0.65	6.24	0.81	165.0
Brass	on actual	0.60	4.98	0.65–0.90	534.0
Copper	product	0.85	n/a	1.20–1.30	542–556.0
Lead	(see Metal	0.00	1.90	0.30	708–711.0
Steel	chapter)	0.00	0.87	0.20	490–495.0
STONE	$/cu. ft.[1]	$/cu. ft.[2]	$/cu. ft.[6]	$/cu. ft.[1]	lbs./cu. ft.[10]
Granite (1" thick; 1 polished face)	80.00	0.00	384.00–720.00	200.00	168.0
Slate (1/4" thick tiles)	100.00	0.00	480.00–720.00	200.00	168.0
Marble (3/4" thick; 1 polished face)	90.00	0.00	400.00–640.00	200.00	160.0
GLASS	$/lb.[1]	$/lb.[2]	$/lb.[7]	$/lb.[1]	lbs./cu. ft.
Window Glass (1/4" thick)	0.45	(0.02)	2.06	0.90	161.0
BRICK	$/each[1]	$/lb.[2]	$/each[9]	$/each[1]	lbs./cu. ft.[10]
Brick, common clay	0.10	0.00	0.62–0.90	0.25–0.50	120.00
Brick, handmade clay	0.20	0.00	n/a	0.80–1.00	150.00
CERAMICS	$/each	$/lb.[2]	$/each	$/each	lbs./cu. ft.[10]
Porcelain	(see ceramics chapter)	0.00	(see ceramics chapter)	(see ceramics chapter)	150.00
Clay tile		0.00			120–150

1 Based on prices from Renovators Resource, Halifax, Nova Scotia, November 1999.

2 Based on prices from Halifax Construction & Debris Recycling Ltd., Halifax, Nova Scotia, November 1999.

3 Based on prices from East Coast Specialty Hardwoods, Halifax, Nova Scotia, November 1999.

4 Based on prices from John Ross & Sons Ltd., Halifax, Nova Scotia, November 1999.

5 Based on prices from W. A. Moir Metals, Halifax, Nova Scotia, November 1999 (for 1/4-inch thick plate stock).

6 Based on prices from Nova Tile and Marble Ltd., Dartmouth, Nova Scotia, November 1999.

7 Based on prices from Kidston Glass, Halifax, Nova Scotia, November 1999 (for 1/4-inch thick glass with unfinished edge).

8 Based on prices from Harbour Metal Recycling Ltd., Dartmouth, Nova Scotia, November 1999 (dependent on season).

9 Based on prices from Shaw Brick Store, Dartmouth, Nova Scotia, November 1999.

10 Based on values from Thomas J. Glover, *Pocket Reference,* 2nd Edition (Littleton, Colo: Sequoia Publishing, 1995).

a Based on purchase price at reuse facility of $1.00/square foot (stock 3/4-inch thick) = $1.33/board foot

b Based on purchase price at reuse facility of $0.75/square foot (stock 3/4-inch thick) = $1.00/board foot

c Based on purchase price at reuse facility of $0.50/square foot (stock 3/4-inch thick) = $0.66/board foot

intended to assist innovators, while at the same time introducing business people, government departments, and the general public to the concept of construction and demolition "waste" recovery. The sequence is based on actual experiences of recycling expert Einar Christensen, and on information gained from others involved with the recovery of building materials and fixtures. It is not intended to be all inclusive, but should help in determining the most cost-effective and environmentally friendly utilization of applicable structures and C&D materials.

It is also important to contribute to the C&D cycle from the opposite end, by reusing found objects wherever and whenever possible. Finding material to reuse can be a fun adventure—in fact, it's sometimes the most fun part of the project. Half of the joy of showing your finished project to a visitor is in telling the story of where the material came from. "I found this in the trash while walking the dog one night" . . . "This came from the old school-house that used to be down on the shore" . . . "This is the old schoolhouse that used to be down on the shore" . . . "Can you believe this used to be a door?" . . . "I found this bronze finish under seven coats of paint" . . . "I built this extra bathroom for half of what I thought it would cost, using these fixtures from the old theater." Whatever the providence or heritage of the piece, it will become part of the story that many will find fascinating. More ideas for where to look for hidden treasure are listed in the sidebar on page 7, and the rest of this book is full of real-life salvage success stories.

When renovating, aim to find a balance between design, ecology, and economy. The reward will be a successful, sustainable project. There is no end to the affliction called resource recycling—when it sets in, one house may not be enough. The urge to sidestep the new materials aisle at the hardware store and dig through the neighborhood trash is infectious. I have realized that my job as a designer and renovator is my hobby, and my hobby is my job.

Basic building materials can be incorporated into an endless variety and scale of projects, many of which are described in this book. Whether you restore, rehabilitate, renovate, remodel, repair, revitalize, rejuvenate, reclaim, renew, replace, refurbish, repaint, repoint, retrofit, reconstruct, replicate, re-erect, rebuild, re-create, redesign, rework, redevelop, or relocate—the key is that all these types of projects involve reusing a material, an object, or a building. By taking a little extra effort to save an element from the past, we can enjoy its presence and continue its life for centuries.

CONSTRUCTION AND DEMOLITION MATERIAL FLOW CHART

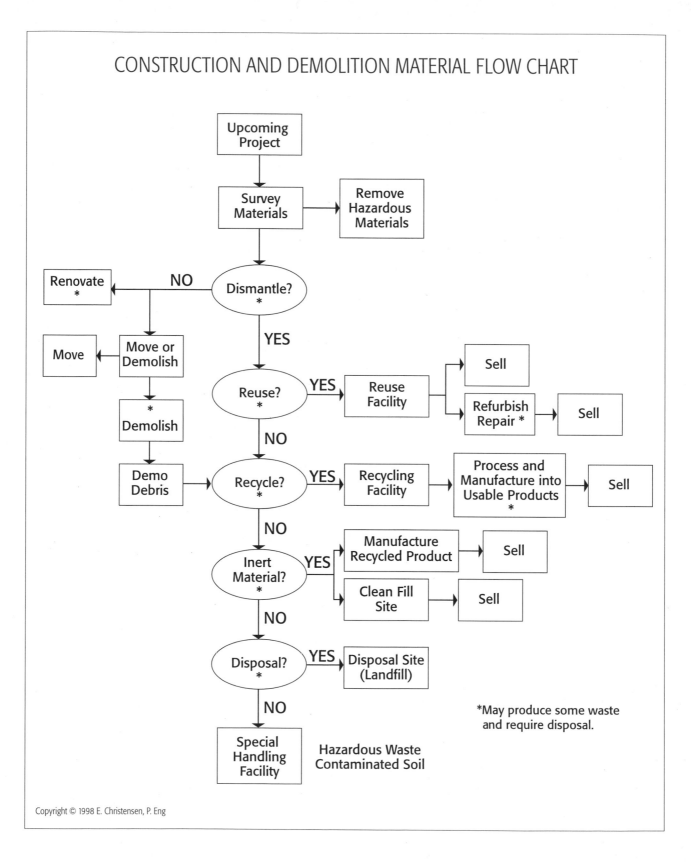

Copyright © 1998 E. Christensen, P. Eng

I have been surprised again and again how creative people can be with a few materials, a little money, and a consciousness of trying to live lightly on Earth. This book shows how many people have created absolute beauty in their homes from the basic building materials—wood, metal, stone, brick, glass, and ceramic—while considering the environment and a budget at the same time. Why not make our efforts worthwhile, beautiful, functional, and good examples for our children and community?

LIKELY SOURCES FOR USED BUILDING MATERIALS

1. **Your Basement.** Your aunt's basement. Your uncle's workshop. Your neighbor's shed. Let people know what you are interested in, and you'll be surprised what will appear out of the dark corners of the storage area.

2. **Flea Markets and Yard Sales.** This is the stuff from the basements of people whom you don't know well enough to ask for directly. You will need to be prepared to accept an item and trust that you can use it. Carry a list of necessary dimensions and a tape measure with you at all times. Rarely will you have the opportunity to return an item if it doesn't fit.

3. **Used Building Material Stores or Salvage Yards.** Many people are making a business out of selling recovered material. Used building material stores are becoming the "Home Depot" of the salvage world, and are full of endless possibilities. Be prepared to pay sales tax, and inquire about refund policies. Many of these stores have Web sites on which you can view digital images and order items without ever having to leave your home. (But this isn't nearly as much fun as combing through all of the other things in the store!) See the resource section for the Used Building Materials Association address. This association carries a listing of their members from across North America.

4. **Renovation and Demolition Sites.** Before you visit these sites, determine exactly what you are looking for and be prepared to deal with people under pressure. Many construction sites are off limits to the public. Some may allow people to view salvageable items, if you are wearing proper safety boots and hats. Other sites may have a viewing room of items open during somewhat irregular hours, so that the public can view the type of material available from the building being demolished. Others may be completely inaccessible with no possibility for salvage. The die-hard salvager needs to be pleasant and persistent, offering up-front cash and assistance in removing requested items.

5. **Material Exchange Listings.** With the growth of the reuse and recycling industries, the Internet now lists a number of exchanges for materials available and materials wanted. Each exchange operates differently: some offer free listings, others charge members to view the site, and some charge a fee for the successful "exchange" of materials. See the resources section for examples.

6. **Newspapers or Secondhand Buyers Guide.** The classified sections of many newspapers include "Building Supplies" or "Building Materials—Used" categories, where homeowners or contractors list their surplus or recently salvaged materials. Prices can be better than at retail outlets, though variety and available sizes may be limited.

POINTS TO CONSIDER WHEN CHOOSING A BUILDING MATERIAL TO REUSE

	DURABILITY	MAINTENANCE	ENVIRONMENTAL BENEFITS/ EMBODIED ENERGY	USER-FRIENDLINESS
WOOD	Strong in compression and tension parallel to grain.	Will rot if continually wet unless sealed or painted.	Provides relief from forestry activity. Prolongs breadth, age, and depth of forests. Can be reused many times before recycling.	Easy to work; similar to new material. Safety measures should be taken to remove old nails.
METAL	Susceptible to rust and corrosion unless coated with protective finish.	Entails preserving (re-oiling, repainting) protective coating on entire surface.	Provides relief from mining and manufacturing new material. Metal industry traditionally not clean nor sustainable environmentally.	Changing the existing shape may require specialized equipment and skills.
STONE	Strong in compression. Lasts longest of all building materials.	Low-maintenance. Interior use may require surface upkeep.	Provides relief from mining new material. Labor value is extended with reuse. Largely dependent on source, location, and transportation.	Resizing may require specialized equipment and skills.
BRICK	Strong in compression; can fail in seismic events.	Will not rot, dent, fade, scratch, peel, or warp.	Provides relief from energy-intensive manufacturing process.	Cleaning off mortar and reuse is simple, but time consuming.
GLASS	Little structural strength. Old glass with waves and bubbles may be weaker.	Easy to clean in most cases.	Provides relief from energy-intensive manufacture. Transportation from few sources is lessened through local reuse.	Easy to replace and cut. Safety glass is more difficult to resize.
CERAMIC	Glazed surfaces provide protection. Generally brittle.	Easy to clean and replace in most cases.	Provides relief from energy-intensive manufacturing process and transportation costs.	Simple tools required for laying mortar bed and trimming tiles. Installing plumbing fixtures may require specialized equipment and skills.

AESTHETICS	REUSABILITY	RECYCLABILITY	COST	AVAILABILITY
Can appear in a variety of finishes, shapes, and dimensions.	Any project requiring wood can use salvaged wood instead of new. Some safety measures should be taken concerning lead paint and foreign metal objects.	Wood chips and sawdust are used for fuel and composite manufacturing.	Usually less than one-half of retail at reuse facilities.	Can be found at most salvage and demolition sites.
Malleability of material provides numerous shapes and forms. Old metalwork is highly sought after.	If the structural integrity has not deteriorated due to rust, cracks, or splits, metals can easily be reused in most applications. Some cutting or welding may be required.	Most metals are recyclable and only require a fraction of the energy to remanufacture.	Largely dependent on object, type of metal, and degree of metalwork involved.	Contractors yards, demolition sites, and landfills are best sources.
Traditionally exudes sign of wealth and permanence. Different colors and faces provide variety of finishes.	Easy to reuse. May be burdensome and expensive to cut and move great distances.	Can be recycled. Market may not support recycling in many regions where new stone is available inexpensively.	Nominal charge for stone, though heavy equipment usage and transportation can be costly.	Contact local demolition firms or salvage operations.
Traditionally popular exterior material. Brick design can be elegant feature.	Can be used in exterior load-bearing walls or cladding, chimneys, fireplaces, floors, patios, walkways. Some types of brick may not be durable in outdoor applications.	Can be tumbled or chipped for use in landscaping.	May be bought for as little as 5¢ per brick if purchaser is willing to clean, stack, and transport.	May be in infrequent supply. Largely dependent on demolitions or large renovations.
Enables light and view planes in buildings. Can become feature in itself. Slight deformities in old glass adds intrigue.	Removal from frames is basic. Resizing glass is easy with simple tools. Thermopanes with broken seals are difficult to reseal.	Recyclable, though inert nature usually limits interest. Some regions recycle glass for drainage and roadbase material.	Can be found for one-quarter to one-half of new equivalent.	Manufactured in few locations, but widely available through renovation and salvage sources.
Variety of shapes, sizes, and colors of tiles enable any desired pattern.	Adhesive used may make it difficult to remove ceramic tiles for reuse. Older fixtures may be incompatible with modern plumbing requirements.	Can be crushed and used as clean fill. Some initiatives are using crushed ceramics in new aggregate mixes.	Largely dependent on object, size, color, and condition. Usually one-quarter to one-half of new.	Wide variety of plumbing fixtures and tiles available at most used building material stores.

Measuring yield from
a tree with a board
footage stick.

Aerial view of a
managed forest.

WOOD

*Only a sweet and
virtuous soul,
Like seasoned timber,
never gives.*

—GEORGE HERBERT

HOW VALUABLE IS WOOD? The answer to this important question is more complicated than it might appear if we look only at the price tag on a 2 x 4 at the lumberyard. We must consider not only how useful and versatile wood is as a building material, but also attempt to take into account the immense amount of energy required to turn a tree in the forest into a usable product. In the introduction, we promised to consider the total life-cycle costs of a product: We need to count the energy required to remove wood from a demolition site and haul it to the landfill by truck, where it will ultimately decompose. All of this energy expended to dispose of a 2 x 4 that could have been salvaged from an old building and reused in a new one.

To make matters even more complicated, the real cost of wood must also include the value of the services that forests provide if we don't cut them down. Forests help mitigate climate, by absorbing heat that would otherwise be reflected back into the atmosphere. They serve as rain traps, filter pollutants from water and air, and prevent soil erosion. Trees provide shade, habitat, and food sources for uncountable other living organisms, including human beings. Trees and other green plants use the Sun's energy to change carbon dioxide (CO_2) into carbohydrates and produce oxygen as a by-product. As plants decay, or are burned, they release the CO_2 back into the atmosphere. Therefore, CO_2 is literally locked up within every piece of lumber that is manufactured. The longer we can use, reuse, and recycle a wood product, the longer we can keep the CO_2 from being emitted back into the atmosphere. According to researchers analyzing air trapped in glacial ice, levels of CO_2 have risen approximately 25 percent since the beginning of the Industrial Revolution. As levels of CO_2 increase, so does global

*The whitewash'd
wall, the nicely
sanded floor,
The varnish'd clock
that click'd behind
the door,
The chest, contriv'd
a double debt to
pay, —
A bed by night, a
chest of drawers
by day.*

—OLIVER GOLDSMITH

warming. It is almost impossible to calculate a dollar value for all the services that forests perform.

When the first European explorers landed in North America, they were met not only by native people, but by a vast mass of wood, impenetrable to the eye. The forests were as thick with trees as the waters were with fish. Unfortunately, since that time we have mishandled both resources, and it is questionable if either will ever rebound sufficiently to sustain our present consumption of them into the new millennium. Although the abundance of wood on the new continent might excuse the rampant exploitation of the resource, in fact, it was the shortage of wood in Europe— because of centuries of overharvesting—that made the extraction of North American timber so economically viable, considering how difficult logging was at that time. Examples of this type of misuse are evident throughout the world. From the fast-disappearing tropical rain forests to the acid-rain damaged Northern Forest, our large tracts of woodland are disappearing.

Yet we continue to refer to wood as a "renewable resource," implying that trees can grow back as quickly as we use them, no

Aerial view of suburban sprawl.

VALUE OF WOOD BUILDING MATERIALS

The first column of this chart shows the price one might expect to receive from a salvage dealer for certain used building materials; the second indicates the price paid or the charge to dispose of the materials at a recycling facility. The next two columns list prices for the material new or used from a reuse facility. Note that in all cases materials are more valuable reused than recycled: a reuse facility pays more than a recycling facility. But the best value is to reuse them for your own projects. The last column shows an estimate of the energy required to extract, transport, and process a raw resource—in this case a tree growing in the forest-into a usable product, such as a plank of tongue-and-groove flooring.

BUILDING MATERIAL	PAID SALVAGE VALUE	PAID (OR CHARGED) TO RECYCLE MATERIAL +/-	NEW MATERIAL PURCHASE PRICE	USED MATERIAL PURCHASE PRICE	DENSITY OF MATERIAL	EMBODIED ENERGY TO CREATE MATERIAL
WOOD	$CAD[1]	$CAD/lb.[2]	$CAD[3]	$CAD[1]	lbs./bd. ft.[4]	BTU/bd. ft.[5]
Flooring, oak t&g/s.f.	1.00	(0.02)	5.00–8.00	3.00–5.00	3.7–4.9	6,633
4 x 4 post, spruce/lin. ft.	0.25	(0.02)	0.90–1.10	1.80	2.3	5,229
Plywood, softwood (4' x 8' sheet, ½" thick)	5.00	(0.02)	29.00	18.00	3.2	14,058

1 Based on prices from Renovators Resource, Halifax, Nova Scotia, November 1999.

2 Based on prices from Halifax Construction & Debris Recycling Ltd., Halifax, Nova Scotia, November, 1999.

3 Based on prices from East Coast Specialty Hardwoods, Halifax, Nova Scotia, November, 1999.

4 Based on values from *Pocket Reference* by Thomas J. Glover, 2nd Edition (Littleton, Colo.: Sequoia Publishing, 1995).

5 Canada Housing and Morgage Corporation, "Optimize," October 1991, p. 5, Table 2.1.

matter how great our demand. The current practice of replacing slow growing species with faster growing coniferous plantations is putting an increased demand on the export and import of hardwoods. Trees have been harvested and replanted throughout this continent. Some ventures have been relatively successful in timing the harvesting and regrowing of trees to meet future expectations, yet massive deforestation has left many scars on mountains and hills that once had trees reaching upward hundreds of feet. We've often filled in the scars with housing developments. These shortsighted practices will require generations to heal Earth's surface, even if we ceased cutting now, and never again will we have such high-quality wood or forests. Our language betrays our egocentricism when we talk about "forest management," and "our resources," implying that we are in control of forests. In reality, we should look at forestry as a partnership. We need the trees more than they need us.

HARVESTING AND MILLING WOOD

Traditional method of hauling timber.

Chainsaw operator. Even one man with a chain saw can fell a tree faster than two with a crosscut saw.

Feller-buncher. Tree harvesting has changed dramatically through the influence of large machinery. Even though a tree can still be cut down with a chain saw or even an axe, we have designed equipment that can cut, strip, and stack a tree in a fraction of the time that it once took. While these new technologies are considered to make logging more "efficient," they also enable us to destroy vast tracts of forest much more quickly than they can grow back.

Loading logs with a forwarder. Even hauling logs out of the forest has changed from horse or oxen to tractors pulling sleds full of stripped trunks. Thousands of miles of logging roads have been blasted into hillsides and across watersheds, further fragmenting forest habitats and causing damaging erosion.

Pond where bark is softened prior to milling. Logs are normally brought to a lumber mill by truck, railway car, barge, or tugboat. Most mills have a pond where logs are stored and sorted prior to being milled. The water helps to soften the bark, which will be stripped off, along with any rough protrusions, prior to being cut. Hundreds of gallons of water are used in the process of milling lumber.

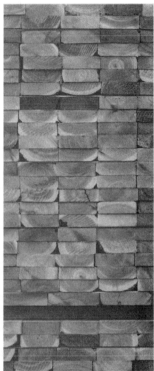

Milled 2 x 6s. Dimension lumber has changed over the years, becoming smaller, and correspondingly weaker. The function of "dressing" lumber means that a lumber mill cleans and softens the edges of the material, making it easier to handle. A finished 2 x 6 is now only $1\frac{1}{2}$ by $5\frac{1}{2}$ inches in cross section.

Sawmill operator taking maximum yield from a tree. In the mill, each log is assessed for the maximum possible yield of board feet, or is milled to specification for certain lumber orders. A sawyer's goal is to take full advantage of the material, and still retain the best grain. Cut lumber is either kiln dried or air dried. After kiln drying, lumber will be "dressed" or planed to final finished size. Air-dried lumber is normally dressed to a larger size prior to drying, so it will dry to the proper dimension.

Transport truck with new logs for utility poles. After the milling and drying process is complete, lumber is transported to local or foreign markets by truck, rail, or ship—often thousands of miles from where the trees originally grew.

USE

It would be extremely time consuming to list all the uses of wood in building construction. Throughout the history of housing, either log, branch, stick, or stud has helped form the skeleton of the building. Wood once even played a role as foundation, plumbing, roofing, and insulation.

Being malleable with a chisel, saw, lathe, or planer, wood has been used in interior and exterior detailing for hundreds of years. Even some early plumbing and rainwater leaders were made of wood. Due to its nature, the only uses in building construction where wood is not a key component is in electrical connections and heating systems—other than as fuel.

THE STRUCTURE, PROPERTIES, AND USES OF MILLED WOOD

The cross-section of a tree. A tree's inner core, or heartwood, consists completely of nonliving cells and is usually differentiated from the outer layer (sapwood) by its darker color. Heartwood is usually denser and more decay resistant than sapwood. Antique heart pine is one of the most sought-after flooring materials. The larger the tree, the more heartwood the log yields.

Century-old weathered shingles. Some types of wood are water repellent, making them an appropriate material for building exteriors. Many shingled structures have withstood decades of freezing rains and strong sun. The cell structure of most woods can absorb and release moisture with little deterioration to the integrity of the material. This is not true in all cases, as mold, decay, and dry rot are among the problems caused by exposing some woods to excessive moisture.

GRAIN

SAPWOOD

HEARTWOOD

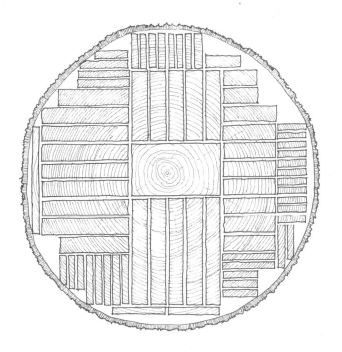

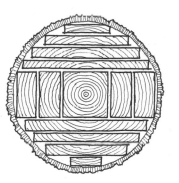

An old-growth tree. This cross-section of a 30-inch-diameter log shows why a larger-diameter log yields more and better lumber than an equivalent volume of smaller trees. More lumber comes from the heartwood, more wide boards can be sawed out, and the wasted wood is minimal compared to the yield.

A 12-inch diameter tree. This diagram represents the typical yield from an average second-growth tree.

An 8-inch log from a quick-growing poplar. The variety and size of lumber available from this log is minimal, with a large amount of wasted wood compared to the yield. Because old-growth trees are no longer available, even softwood lumber in wide and long lengths is sold at a premium; therefore shorter lengths, finger-jointed, and laminated softwood products have captured a larger market share. The use of lumber from smaller trees changes the appearance of the finished piece.

Compression, tension, shear, and bending stresses. Wood has excellent compression, tension, shear, and bending strength. When compressed parallel to its grain, wood fibers resist loads by giving lateral support to one another. The compressive strength of wood actually reaches its maximum when it is compressed to about one-third of its original volume. Wood is also strong in tension parallel to the grain. Due to the continuous fibers in many species, wood is also very strong in shear perpendicular to the grain, as the diagram illustrates. Bending loads create compressive stress on the top of the wood member, and tensile loads on the bottom. Wood performs very well in most bending applications.

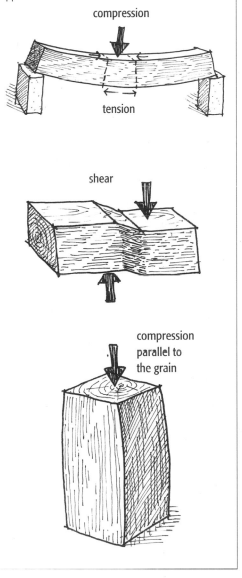

CHARACTERISTICS AND USES OF HARDWOODS AND SOFTWOODS

The terms *softwood* and *hardwood* are misleading. Certain hardwoods, such as basswood or poplar, are softer than the average softwood, while some softwoods, such as southern pine and Douglas fir, are harder than several of the hardwoods. Softwoods, also called conifers, usually bear cones and have needle-like leaves that stay green throughout the winter and remain on the tree for two or more years. Hardwoods, or deciduous trees, have broad leaves that turn color in the fall and are shed from the tree.

SOFTWOODS

SPECIES	CHARACTERISTICS	COLOR	USE
CEDAR, WESTERN RED	Very durable and resistant to fungi and rodents. Lightweight.	Reddish brown which weathers to a silver gray.	Exterior siding, roof shingles, venetian blinds, closets, and chests.
CEDAR, EASTERN WHITE	Light and decay resistant, tough under impact. Brittle and low-shrinkage rate.	Pale brown to nearly white.	Fence posts, shingles, canoe construction.
DOUGLAS FIR	Straight grained with a tendency for a spiral, wavy grain. Difficult to work yet strong and available in long lengths and long sections. Does not paint well.	Pink to light reddish brown.	Structure, flooring, doors, trim.
HEMLOCK	Usually straight grained and fairly even textured. Stains and paints well. Not durable under wet/dry conditions.	Pale brown with distinct growth rings.	Structure, joinery, paneling, furniture, flooring.
LARCH	Straight grained, very durable, and tough. Harder than pine, very resinous and difficult to stain.	Reddish brown heartwood with a yellowish-white sapwood.	Planking, heavy construction, fencing, poles, gates, flooring, furniture, windows, doors.
PINE	Good durable timber, easy to work. Rich in resin. Must be sealed before being stained or treated.	Varies from white, to red, to yellow.	Furniture, paneling, windows, interior and exterior doors, exterior siding.
SPRUCE	Straight grained and tends to splinter. Stains, paints, and varnishes well. Resistant to weather, fungi, and insects.	White to pink.	Timbers, beams, siding, flooring, planking, joinery.

HARDWOODS

SPECIES	CHARACTERISTICS	COLOR	USE
ASH	Straight fine grain, even texture. Seasons well, water resistant. Comparatively light, soft, and easy to work.	Light red to orange brown.	General woodturning, axe handles, plywood.
BEECH	Knot-free with flecked grain pattern, giving a uniform and attractive finish. Exceptionally strong timber able to bend and turn.	White to pale brown with tendency to darken to a reddish brown with exposure to light.	Furniture (chairs, desks), veneers, doors, flooring.
BIRCH	Fine texture, often mixed with maple for flooring.	White to light brown.	Furniture (upholstery framing), doors, turnery, flooring.
ELM	Good bending properties. Very resistant to splitting due to cross grain, and highly water resistant.	Brown.	Furniture, cabinetry, chairs, coffins, boatbuilding, flooring.
MAPLE	Fine wavy grain known as "Bird's Eye" maple. Strong and durable.	Creamy white, often with reddish tinge.	Furniture, tabletops, flooring.
OAK	Can corrode ironwork due to gallic acid. Strong, durable, and impermeable. Grows quickly. Somewhat susceptible to insects. Good replacement for mahogany or teak. Polishes well.	Can vary from yellowish brown with distinct broad rays giving a "silver-grain" effect to American "Red" oak.	All types of interior finish, window sills, fascias, doors, fencing, furniture, flooring.
POPLAR	Lightweight, tough. Not liable to splinter. Woolly grain that may stain in patches if exposed to moisture.	Light in color; white, gray and pale red brown.	Shelving, interior joinery, turnery, and plywood.
WALNUT	Grain from straight to slightly wavy. Coarse texture may have irregular streaks or a striped effect.	Depending on source can be rich, dark brown, to grayish brown to a light, pinkish brown.	Decorative veneer, furniture, and plywood.

REUSE

Wood is one of the easier building materials to reuse. The most efficient method of reusing building material is to leave it in its original location. This may sound simplistic, but think of the time and money that you can save by redesigning a renovation project to reuse the existing materials. You save the time necessary to dismantle the material and transport it to the landfill, and the exhorbitant tipping fees to dispose of the waste. It is also expensive to replace the original wood with a virgin material. The next few pages illustrate several innovative techniques for reusing whole buildings. The following section describes the even wider range of possibilities for salvaging different wood items for reuse either in their existing form, or for processing for other uses.

Time-lapse of roof raising. A renovation contractor was able to save time and money for the homeowners, who wanted to increase the usable floor space on their home's second floor. They gained approximately 30 percent of the floor area by literally lifting the roof. They disconnected the lower end of the rafters and cut the side walls so that the roof hinged, then inserted new support walls below. They raised the roof, shingles and all, with jacks, and installed a ridge beam at the peak.

Moving Buildings

Relocating a building is often seen as a Superman stunt, possible only with modern technology, but documentation shows that some buildings in the United States were moved as early as the eighteenth century. Relocation is actually a fairly common occurrence. Most houses that are moved are slated for demolition because they stand in the way of a proposed widening of a highway or some other type of large-scale construction project. Houses are also relocated because of recurring floodplain damage, neighborhood rezoning, or commercial development. Eroding shorelines can force homeowners to move their house back from the water's edge or onto another property. Occasionally, historically important houses are moved to a more desirable site or to create an historical district elsewhere.

Sometimes buildings can be bought inexpensively, either for back taxes or for a low bid at auction. On average, a house can be moved for one-half to two-thirds the replacement cost of a comparable new house. The cost to transport the building in one piece is dependent on the distance moved, as well as its size and structural considerations.

The key to moving a building successfully is to work with a company that has had years of experience. Such a company will have the considerable amount of specialized equipment needed to do the job properly. They will also be insured against unforeseen and other liabilities. Look for listings in your *Yellow Pages* under "House and Building Movers."

House floating down the Atlantic Coast. A barge can be used to float a building to its new location. This was a frequent practice of many communities dependent on a waterway for fishing, lumbering, or shipping. It has the benefits of not tying up roadways and avoiding costs of raising electrical lines. In Newfoundland, as work along the shore changed due to the fishery and forestry, houses were literally floated up and down the Atlantic Coast, in and out of bays and inlets.

SAVING BECK HOUSE

Sandra Strain and Lorin Brehaut, natives of Prince Edward Island, discovered firsthand that moving a building can be an interesting and rare experience. They had inquired about buying an abandoned ancestral home, known as the Beck house, which was owned by a neighbor who wanted the building removed by whatever means possible, even if it meant burning it down. Lorin and Sandra purchased "Beck," including the cut sandstone blocks used in the foundation walls, for $6,000 Canadian (CAD).

In the meantime, Lorin and Sandra had purchased another family relic, the Brehaut house, a late eighteenth-century house on the eastern shores of the Island. They were in a quandary: They now owned two houses, but the cost of a second well and septic tank was beyond their financial means. They decided to move the Beck

House the half-mile down the road and connect it to the Brehaut house. As Sandra explained,

It was an opportunity that we couldn't pass up—not only because this was a building of one of our ancestors—the fact is, this is a well-built building with so much character, warmth, and appeal, we just couldn't let it be demolished. Even though it appears to need some careful attention, it is a financially smarter idea to start with this building, than to build a new one from the ground up.

The costs for this effort were minimal, in return for the value of the building, though Sandra would say that it took more time than anticipated. Just the short move from less than a mile away involved the telephone company, the cable company, the power company, and the Department of Transportation and Public Works—to make sure a culvert was strong enough to take the load. A building permit and a moving permit were required for the event. Sandra admits that the coordination of the move and organizing five permits prior to the move was comparable to performing an athletic feat. The actual move took less than an hour, and was completed without any problems.

Beck House and Brehaut House united. The Beck House was built in 1870 in the Maritime Vernacular style. It has a gabled dormer above the front door, which has a beautiful transom window, called a fanlight. The house never had electricity and most of the original interior still remains. Birchbark insulation was found in the roof structure during a reshingling some years ago.

Salvaging Wood

Interest in wood salvage is growing for a number of reasons: used materials are often only half the cost of new, the quality of used materials often exceeds that of new manufactured products (such as with pine plank flooring), and the design and style of reclaimed materials can match the styles of a home being renovated. Wood can be more easily separated and removed for reuse than stone or brick, being lighter and more forgiving to a crowbar or other tools. Wood is also one of the simpler materials to work with using familiar tools and techniques. Another motivational factor is that reworking outdated pieces into a usable form provides a creative outlet. For the environmental renovator, making something out of a material diverted from a landfill can be doubly rewarding.

Garden gate from salvaged Douglas fir timbers. The talented designer and builder Peter Tomlin built this garden gate with timbers from the rubbish pile of a demolished wharf warehouse. The gate protects the entrance of a commercial flower and herb garden from a busy road. Peter made a heavy tongue-and-groove joint in the timbers and pegged them together using hardwood dowels; he used no nails in the construction of the gate! The top arch is a steel ring from a wagon wheel, split apart to span the opening. The large hinges made by local blacksmith Ian Hope-Simpson take into account the immense weight of the doors.

Salvaged timbers used in a new home. The G. R. Plume Company in Ferndale, Washington, salvaged the Douglas fir timber from a warehouse demolition for this new home on Lummi Island. The timber frame may be more expensive than standardized wood framing in a new home, but the aesthetics and quality of the building are far superior.

Gordon Plume has also been very involved with the testing and grading of salvaged timber. Many early buildings with salvageable wood frames do not automatically meet building codes, even though they often contain a better-quality material. Without a mill's grade stamp, any salvaged timber is required to have an engineer's stamp or letter, approving their use in structural applications. Plume is working with various lumber agencies to test what effect holes, notches, and paint have on the acceptance of salvaged timbers in new construction.

Flooring from salvaged lumber can add a very attractive feature to a new home, or can integrate well into a renovation.

Softwood flooring planks can be found up to 24 inches wide, though at a premium price. The trees from which these boards came were most likely first-generation growth with large diameter trunks. Planking widths average 4 inches to 10 inches, and generally a variety of widths and lengths best suit a laid floor. It is best if planks are long enough to cover the entire width of a room, as plank widths will not exactly match when laid end-to-end. Commonly available softwoods include pine, spruce, fir, and hemlock. Homes built over a century ago would likely have had spruce and pine planks laid interchangeably. A fir floor will have a considerably different grain and color.

Most salvaged hardwood flooring is available at between one-half to equal the price of new hardwood flooring. Remember that if you replaced the longer, knot-free lengths with identical new material, it would be at least two to three times as expensive—if you could find it at all. Generally, salvaged flooring will be much longer and will give the finished product a quality appearance, as most new hardwood flooring pieces are shorter than four feet.

PUT YOUR FOOT DOWN: SALVAGED FLOORING IDEAS

Salvaged beams to be milled into plank flooring; a portable sawmill; and milled planking. The salvaged flooring business is well-established on the North American east coast. With many one- to two-century-old buildings being demolished to make room for more modern, efficient ones, a huge quantity of large timbers and flooring is being salvaged. Most of this material is of higher quality than the new material that would replace it. The boards are longer, mostly knot-free, and are stable in terms of warping, bending, or cupping. Many companies mill old timbers into new flooring.

SALVAGED
FLOORING
IDEAS

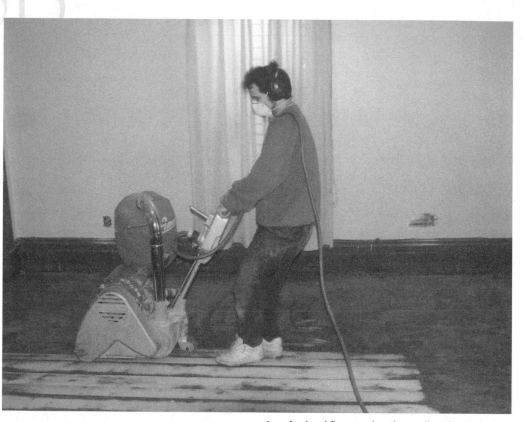

A professional floor sander. The sanding of a salvaged hardwood floor should be undertaken only by a person with patience and considerable upper body strength. You can rent sanding equipment from most construction equipment rental stores. Consult with a professional floor sander prior to taking on the job, as their experience and speed at completing the job may be competitive with your learning curve. Whichever route you choose, ensure that everyone in the vicinity of the sander is wearing a proper respirator. Potential hazards created from sanding floors include dust from lead and other airborne chemicals.

Stained, surface planed, and painted planking. Salvaged softwood flooring can be stained, painted, planed, or left with its existing finish, depending on the intended use. Most water-based finishes are as durable as oil-based finishes and either can be used on softwood floors. An oil-based finish tends to "warm up" or yellow the color of the wood, whereas a water-based finish does not. As well, the odors resulting

from the offgassing of oil-based finishes will take a few days to dissipate. Some people choose to stain softwood flooring, though a clear finish shows the character and quality of the wood best. Some defects, such as nail holes, knots, insect scars, and variations in color may be evident on salvaged softwood planks. Depending on their use, these defects can add an antique quality to the floor.

Removing hardwood flooring. Use a flat crowbar or hammer to salvage hardwood flooring by carefully prying up the full length of each piece, starting from the edge with the tongue exposed.

Cleaning tongue-and-groove with a paint scraper. Hardwood flooring that has been heavily used and finished numerous times will require some additional preparation prior to re-laying it. Using a scraper, remove all dirt and accumulated debris from the top of the tongue. This will aid in re-laying the floor as tightly as possible, which is necessary for hardwood.

Salvaged hardwood flooring. Salvaged hardwood is highly recommended for use in a new home or renovation. The more common hardwoods used at the turn of the century were birch, maple, oak, and cherry. Used building material stores usually sell reclaimed hardwood in 10- or 20-square-foot bundles. Most tongue-and-groove hardwood flooring is approximately 3/4- to 7/8-inch thick.

SAFETY ALERT

The main difficulty with using power tools on salvaged wood is that nails or other foreign objects may be embedded in a plank or hidden under layers of paint or other finishes. These can be vey dangerous if not removed with the utmost care. A metal detector can be purchased for as little as $100. It should be used repeatedly after each discovered nail is removed. Removing the nails can also be tricky, as many old nails can break off and leave pieces embedded in the wood. If some metal still remains in the plank, cut around the area and recycle the piece that is unsuitable for reuse.

SALVAGED FLOORING IDEAS

Salvaged plank flooring and hand-hewn beams in new home. Many people have been surprised to learn that this home is brand new. The homeowners chose to incorporate salvaged flooring and beams to add warmth and character throughout their house. The softwood planks vary from 6 to 16 inches wide. Reclaimed hand-hewn beams can be graded for structural use, though these are attached to the ceiling as a decorative element.

HOW TO MAKE A PLUGGED-SCREW CONNECTION

1. Clamp the wood pieces together and drill pilot holes.

2. Countersink ½-inch-deep holes with a ⅜-inch drill bit.

3. Connect the wood pieces with 1½- to 2 inch-long #8 screws.

4. Fill the holes with ⅜-inch wood plugs. Use wood glue for a secure fit. Wipe excess glue from the surface of wood after inserting each plug. Use a hammer or mallet to lightly tap each plug into the countersunk holes. Let the plug sit out slightly from the surface.

5. When dry, sand the plugs flush with the wood surface. Finish as desired.

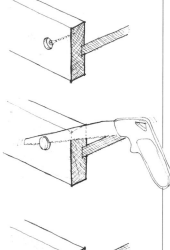

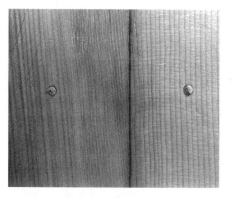

Nailed and Plugged-Screw Connections. Several different methods can be used to fasten softwood planks to the subfloor. The easiest is to face-nail each board with common nails. Use a nail set to drive these nails ⅛ inch beneath the surface of the boards, so the nailheads will not obstruct a sander.

The second method is to countersink holes into the planks and pilot drill holes for screws to connect the planks to the subflooring. Cover the screwheads with wooden plugs made from the same type of wood, or from a contrasting colored wood. Set the plugs in place with glue. Sand when dry.

Salvaged softwood plank wardrobe.
Salvaged floor planking is also perfectly suited for cabinetry. The planks are stable, thick, and full of character. Tom Livingston, a talented sustainable builder and cabinetmaker, fabricated this wardrobe completely from salvaged material. The wood, purchased from a used building material store, has many wonderful knots and marks, which add character to the finished product. The hardware, hinges, door pulls, and lock are from salvaged hardware as well. The most interesting design feature of the cabinet is that the self-leveling feet are actually cast-iron doorknobs mounted on threaded metal shanks.

WHEN IS A DOOR NOT A DOOR?

Wooden doors, window frames, columns, and other trimwork are all versatile pieces to reuse in renovation projects or furniture building. Inspect doors and windows for their thermal efficiency. Generally, single-pane windows and wooden doors are not adequate as the only protection from the outdoors. Incorporate them into a storm porch or air-lock entry where a more energy-efficient second door protects your home from heat loss.

Salvaged wooden door in new construction. This old wooden paneled door was incorporated into a new Nantucket-style home. The door opens into a vestibule where a second door goes into the heated kitchen.

Door hinges used for drawer pulls. Cut cast iron hinges serve as the drawer pulls for the chest of drawers. The cabinet has dovetailed joinery and well-proportioned drawers.

A bedframe and cabinet from salvaged doors. Michael Gorman, a building dismantler and talented woodworker, wants to see how many possible furniture pieces he can create from old wooden doors. "I like the challenge of building a necessary piece of furniture with limited tools and materials. The quality of the door inspired me to make something solid yet elegant." Mike used three doors for this majestic bedframe. The side rails are comprised of a four-panel door split lengthwise. Additional storage space is incorporated under the futon.

PANELED DOOR BENCH

A unique use for an old paneled door is in the creation of a door bench. Only one four-paneled door was required to build this entire bench, ingeniously using all of the panels in the design. Use a solid-paneled door, at least 1½ inches thick, along with scrap 2 x 4 and 2 x 2 (to support the bench at front, back, and sides). The construction is simple using a plugged-screw connection (see page 28). You will need a circular saw or table saw to cut the door, and a jigsaw to make the curved side of the bench. Use this bench indoors, as water will deteriorate the molding, paneling, and connections.

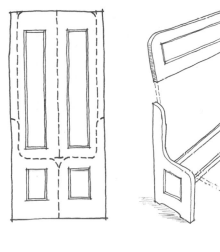

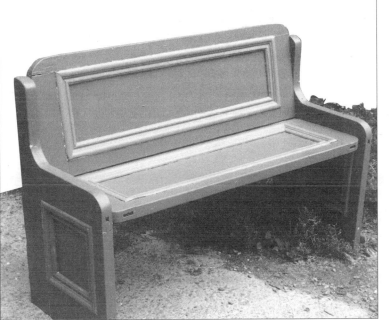

SAFETY ALERT

Lead was used in paint prior to the 1970s to give a lighter tone and more durability. The concern with sanding lead-painted objects is that fine airborne particulates can be inhaled and cause lead poisoning. As well, continued exposure to lead from direct contact or ingestion can be harmful. Even though the outer layer of paint on an object may not contain lead, it is very difficult to identify lead paint under many layers. Lead paint testing kits are available from most paint stores. Some environmental and health agencies recommend that families with young children repaint any old surfaces below 3 feet high with a lead-free paint.

HEADBOARD FROM OLD PANELED DOOR

An easy and affordable way to accent your bed with a grand-looking headboard is to use a solid-paneled door. This old door was purchased at a used building material store. Panel number and configurations vary, though the best door style is one that has equal-length horizontal panels, as this five-panel door/headboard demonstrates. The headboard is finished with a piece of 1 x 4 planking and crown molding. Level and position the headboard carefully so that a ledge is not in the wrong place for sitting up in bed. The easiest method to attach the headboard is with angle brackets and screws. Use a studfinder to ensure adequate support. Paint if desired.

OTHER INTERIOR IDEAS

WINDOW FRAME POT RACK

An affordable method to add interest to a room is to hang elements from the ceiling, varying the perceived ceiling height. Wooden elements with interesting shapes and finishes work well in the kitchen, studio, bedroom, dining room, and bathroom—anywhere that objects can be displayed or stored. Susan and I suspended this large window sash, with the glass removed, from the ceiling with S-hooks and four lengths of chain. Screw threaded hooks into the underside of the sash to provide a method to hang pots and pans. Anything from dried flowers, mobiles, or wind chimes to cookware can be hung below. Items such as wooden crates, linens, boxes, and sports equipment can be stored on top of the window, as long as the ceiling anchor, chain, and sash are capable of supporting those items. Wooden ladders are also great items to use in place of a window sash.

SHUTTER SHELF

Interior and exterior shutters were once used to control visibility and security, without cutting off air flow into a home. Wooden shutters were built with operable or fixed louvers, and might be painted, stained, or varnished. Shutters can be found in abundance in the basements of the old houses that used to be adorned with them, at flea markets and salvage stores, or even with the curbside garbage. Be sure to choose shutters that aren't warped or split.

This shelf, made from two equal-length interior shutters, is very easy to assemble and is great for storage of small collectibles and glassware. Each shelf is a square piece of planking with an angled cut for the exposed edge. Attach the shelf to the shutters with screws from the rear side of the shutter.

Spindles and newels. Newel posts are among the more interesting remnants from century-old homes. These carved and turned short posts were made from both hardwood and softwood. Often it will be difficult to reincorporate old newels into a new stair system, as many building codes require taller supports and handrails for safety reasons. As well, many of the large newel posts found at architectural antique stores or used building material stores won't look proportionately correct in new stair systems, since the large entries and stairways of some of the grand homes of the past have been replaced by more compact vestibules with lower ceilings. But a newel post reused in another situation not only becomes a visual centerpiece, but also salvages an out-of-date relic from the past. You can reuse stairtreads, spindles, and banisters in new construction, as long as you adhere to all building codes.

Newel post Bible stand. Often, spindles and newel posts can be used as legs for furniture. Ernie Hicks, an ingenious wood-worker, used a newel post to build this Bible or dictionary stand.

SPINDLE TABLE

The legs of this sturdy side table were made from salvaged spindles from a century-old staircase. The top of the table is made from softwood plank flooring carefully removed from a circa 1905 house demolition. Use a handsaw and mitre box to make clean angled cuts for the narrow molding that edges the plank top. You can also use molding to build a skirt to support the tabletop. The spindle legs easily attach to the skirt. We used a popular old-time recipe to finish this table: equal parts boiled linseed oil, melted beeswax, and turpentine, applied with a soft cloth in repeated thin coats until the finish was even and smooth.

Cabinets salvaged from a hospital demolition.
Replacing cabinetry is one of the most common home renovation projects. Often the cabinetry is completely removed, or minimally the doors are replaced. Most cabinetry can be used again, in different projects. As well, many commercial and institutional buildings undergo renovations, including replacing their cabinetry. Institutional cabinetry is generally of high quality and lasts longer than most residential cabinetry. You can take advantage of used cabinets to make the renovation more affordable.

This attractive kitchen has reincorporated wooden base cabinets salvaged from a hospital demolition site. The homeowners painted the cabinets dark blue, and used pine planks as the countertop for the kitchen island. The hinged folding table on the front of the island is also a pine plank. (To learn more about this renovation project, see "The $1,000 Kitchen," page 152.)

Wooden mantle. Fireplace mantels are interesting design pieces that are often removed from older homes, as open-hearth fireplaces tend not to be energy efficient. As well, the fireplaces are often closed off or removed when older homes are subdivided into apartments. The result is that many mantels are available for reuse. If you are not looking specifically for a fireplace mantel, these decorative pieces can also be used as headboards, store counter fronts, or lintels for doorways or displays.

Molding box. Molding and trim can be reused as picture frames, mirror frames, small boxes, and a variety of other items.

Decorative brackets. Exterior trimwork brackets from from old houses make perfect shelf supports in a home. The ornate designs and curvy forms make a unique addition to a decor. These brackets, newly made from old lumber, are patterned from early Victorian entry porch supports.

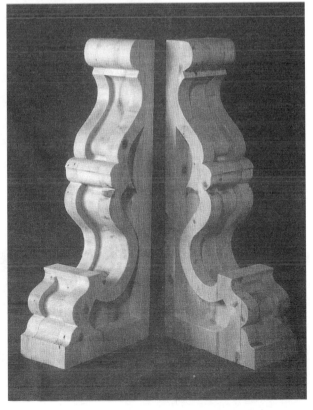

A variety of molding, trim, and rosettes. Hang on to all the trim and molding from your home during renovation. Trying to match older molding designs with new material can be a costly and difficult challenge. Painted moldings can be costly and time-consuming to strip. Lightly scrape and sand the molding in a well-ventilated area, wearing a proper respirator (a precaution if dealing with lead paint), and prime the molding to be repainted.

RECYCLING

When wood is removed from a building and cannot be reused, it can still be recycled as waste wood. However, a variety of contaminants make some wood nonrecyclable. It is more difficult to recycle wood that has been painted several times, as some woods are coated with lead-based paint. Creosote and preserved wood treatments (copper, chromium, arsenic, formaldehyde, and pentachlorophenol) are detrimental to human health and to the environment. As well, wooden items such as railway ties, telephone poles, marine pilings, and fence posts may contain polynuclear aromatic hydrocarbons (PAHs) and are not recommended for reuse in construction. Banning these chemicals and preservatives for such purposes will assist us in establishing a more successful strategy to reuse and recycle all wood.

It is difficult to deal with contaminated wood as a waste material. Some regions do not allow this wood to be burned in an incinerator because of potential emission problems. In other areas, dis-

A mountain of wood shavings. Large amounts of sawdust and shavings are produced during the production of wood products. This material can be recycled by using it as the primary source for manufacturing particleboard, and MDF (medium-density fiberboard). The shavings can be used for animal bedding and landscaping. Bark is also mulched for landscaping purposes. This material is generally easy to market, as it has not yet been contaminated, nor has it been previously processed. Similar to sawdust recycling, the vast amounts of offcuts and bark from the milling process can be used for hog fuel, wood pellets, or the

FROM STUMP TO DUMP: COMPLETING THE CYCLE

manufacture of other wood products. Willamette Industries, a particleboard facility in Eugene, Oregon, certifies that its product has a 10 percent minimum recycled content, including clean wood from construction sites and sawmill offcuts.

Wood debris ready for processing. Recent improvements to the machinery that recycles used building material make wood waste very useful. Heavy sorters, crushers, and grinders are required to reduce large volumes of wood to smaller sizes.

Grinder/chipper making mulch. Another interesting use for recycled wood waste is the wood mulch industry. A wood-fiber mulch designed for hydraulic seeding and erosion control is sought after in many regions. Grass seed is mixed with the wood fiber and then packaged. This product is becoming popular in the huge lawn-patch market.

This piece of equipment processes wood up to 10 feet long. The horizontal grinder has a screen that retains the material in the grinder until it can pass through the required grid size. A large magnet situated at the discharge end of the conveyor seizes foreign metal objects, such as nails and spikes, that can damage the equipment, or limit the uses of the processed material. This equipment is very expensive to operate, so any salvage and reuse that can be done prior to this process will minimize operational costs.

posal of such material has been banned, due to the leaching problems of the chemicals into adjacent water and soil. As a method to reduce the volumes of wood going to landfills, some regions are attempting to implement wood recycling programs. Recycled wood can be combined with other recycled products to make a variety of products including particleboard, sandwich panels, wall paneling, kitchen cabinetry, and fiberboard.

Many manufactured wood products use wood fiber, chips, and sawdust as a primary feedstock. Waste timber, and waste from the milling process, is used to manufacture many composite board products. Sadly, in order to keep up with the demand for these composite materials, some feedstock comes from new timber grown in quick-growth forests. The perception may be that composites are inferior to solid lumber, but they can be affordable, have high dimensional stability, and are becoming a popular means of using recycled material. The most common product is medium-density fiberboard (MDF), which is the basis for most cabinetry on the market today. The quality of MDF can vary, specifically because of the type of binder, or glue, used to bind the wood particles together.

Solid timbers for beams, joists, studs, and stringers in structural capacities have been replaced by smaller-dimensioned pieces. The same is also true for nonstructural components such as lintels,

COMPLETING
THE CYCLE

Wood trusses with small wood members. Recycling can also occur once wood has been sawn into dimensional lumber. Offcuts—short pieces usually under two feet in length—are produced during the milling process or on a construction site. Trusses built from offcuts, gang-nailed with plates for strength and security, are common within the residential and light commercial construction industry.

particleboard, and plywood. Again, this is a well-established industry that utilizes smaller trees and wood waste for manufacture. While this trend to switch to composite wood products uses material that might previously have been waste, it does make it more difficult to introduce used or salvaged material into new construction.

One of the largest existing markets for recycled wood is as a fuel. Many commercial boiler operators use recycled wood as an affordable alternative to new wood fuel stock. Although wood is a relatively clean-burning fuel, with little harmful emissions such as sulfur dioxide, many people argue that burning material is not recycling. Wood-burning pellet stoves have become quite popular. This has spurred the availability of wood pellets as a fuel source. The pellet industry started about ten years ago in the western United States, in response to environmental concerns. It takes about two tons of sawdust to produce one ton of pellets. In 1991, it was estimated that within the province of Nova Scotia (population 900,000), approximately 440,000 tons of waste, including sawdust, bark, chips, slabwood, and shavings, were generated at sawmills. This was one of the reasons for a local company to design and build a wood pellet plant based on several North American plant designs.

As we become more environmentally aware, we are beginning to realize the true life span of some building materials. If the current salvaged material market is cyclical and we are now reusing one hundred-year-old materials, how will the salvaged materials market look in fifty years? Will the materials we are now building with come apart easily to be used again and again? Why are we using adhesives and nail guns to join materials when we know they will be difficult to separate later? Deteriorated particleboard and laminated materials are being stripped from buildings after only ten or fifteen years, due to poor performance and outdated styles. The salvage industry should prepare for the onslaught of plastics, vinyls, and wood composites entering the market, replacing solid wood, metal, and glass—and consumers should try to account for life-cycle costs and reuse potential when they purchase new wood products.

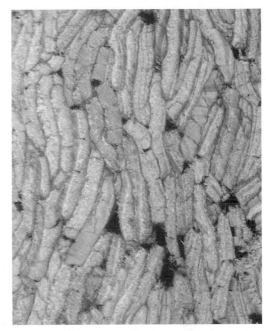

End grain of parallel strand lumber. New products such as parallel strand lumber and laminated veneer lumber (LVL) take a strong position in replacing solid lumber. Parallel strand lumber is made by staggering the lengths of small wood strips, then bonding them together in a microwave curing process. It is highly rated, because it has no knots or splits to limit its structural capabilities.

Another use for recycled wood is within the relatively new industry of "plastic woods." Plastic woods, such as Timbrex, are made from two recycled materials: wood and polystyrene. They have a market in nonstructural applications where fire code ratings are not required. Plastic wood has been used in the construction of docks, fencing, benches, and playground equipment. This material is decay resistant and not susceptible to breakdown by UV rays.

CHRIS SMITH'S "JAMIESON IRISH HOUSE & GRILL"

Chris Smith returned to his family neighborhood of Dartmouth, Nova Scotia, after being away for twenty years. His dream was to build a true neighborhood pub—an upscale tap room offering premium spirits. He wanted to create a fun place from scratch, using lots of old items, incorporating bold textures and colors in a comfortable setting.

Having hobby construction skills, a passion for antiques, and an interest in scavenger hunting, Chris found this a great challenge and experience. "I enjoy making something from nothing. I've always had fun converting objects into other things. At home I've got a lobster crate as the base for a table, and a couple of old leather suitcases form another table."

Chris Smith at his Jamieson Irish House and Grill bar.

Two separate lounge areas have inviting leather sofas surrounded by an old wrought iron handrail.

It's all in the details. An actual gabled dormer with a fanlight design, supported by two tall white pillars, creates an archway at the rear of the bar. These pieces were all salvaged from a turn-of-the-century home.

Jamieson Irish House and Grill is the result of all of Chris's energy and enthusiasm. This 2,100-square foot establishment is located in an unlikely setting—a strip mall! Even the bland setting of the mall didn't discourage Chris. In fact, it makes the transformation more delightful. As you walk in the front doors, you leave a twentieth-century setting for an earlier era. Inside the vestibule, Chris has utilized an old louvered door and a twelve pane window as a contrast to the glass and steel exterior doors.

Many salvaged items have been incorporated into the bar. The bar itself is of bold construction, glowingly warm in color. Three salvaged doors, positioned horizontally, form the front base of the bar, and two early Victorian newel posts between the doors extend above the countertop. The rear of the bar consists of more salvaged doors, cut in half and positioned vertically to make high upper cabinets. The back surface of the shelves consists of old tongue-and-groove softwood wainscoting. Chris bought lots of reclaimed door trim, rosettes, baseboard, and crown molding to finish most of the interior millwork. Salvaging doors not only creates a turn-of-the-century aesthetic, it also saves money. "Most people don't notice the wainscot on the entire perimeter of the bar is actually salvaged paneled doors," Smith says with a money-saving smile. He attached twelve doors, purchased for only $5 each, horizontally on the wall. New wall paneling couldn't have been installed for less, and the panel and molding detail in the old doors creates instant charm and character.

The tables are custom built using salvaged 9-inch-wide spruce planks. All the flooring is salvaged, rough-hewn 3-inch-wide maple boards. Each washroom stall sports a 36-inch-wide door. Toilets and pedestal sinks were bought from a liquidated building material store. Chris suspended an

old door between the urinal and sink to ensure privacy in the men's washroom. An old chicken coop door stands behind the sink, with a small mirror where the original window would have been. Even hardware, door closers, and doorknobs used throughout the establishment are salvaged.

Some materials had to be bought new—leather chairs, bar chairs, china, lumber, drywall, plumbing hardware, and paint. The financing was a balancing act. Smith's approach was to invest money on the surfaces that would be touched, and less on those that would only be seen. His scavenging skills, and an Internet search led him to fifty-three chairs at $20 each in New York. On his trip to pick them up, he traded forty-six lobster traps that he had purchased for $5 each for an antique Coke fridge priced at $690, which has become a real attraction in the bar. Other trade-offs were also interesting. Chris has calculated that one of the chairs from New York cost the same as one new plate, and five leather chairs cost twenty times more than the bar. This approach follows Smith's "theory of surfaces that will get touched," and somehow the balance works.

Chris also invested in skilled trades where he needed them. He hired a lead carpenter, a plumber, and an electrician. Another investment was to commission Mike Lewis of Halifax to complete a floor-to-ceiling painting of a mid-1800s street scene in Ireland. Chris's need to build affordably has resulted in fine, quality work. It's definitely a success. The popularity of the bar has already attracted not only a returning clientele, but also magazine writers and much publicity.

When asked whether going this route took extra effort, Chris's reply was that he had no trouble incorporating old with new; they blend absolutely beautifully. "By function of what I wanted to create, this was the only affordable route to getting my business off the ground."

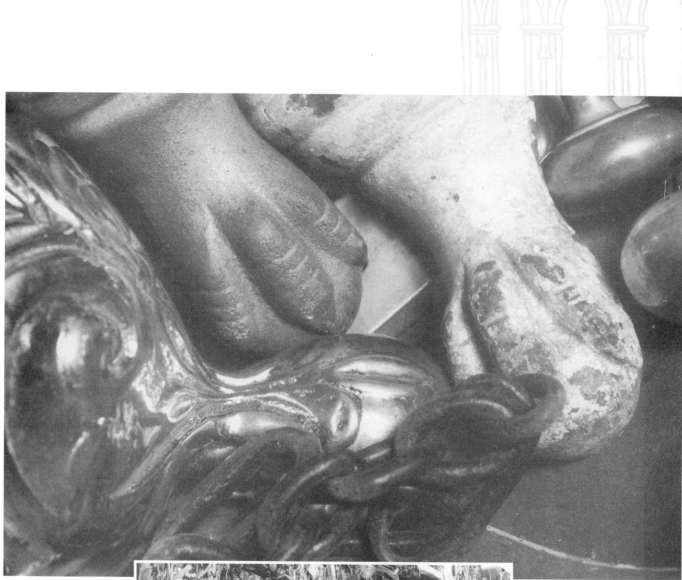

Cast-iron bathtub feet,
chain, and doorknobs.

Metal at the recycler's,
ready for processing.

METAL

IT WOULD HAVE BEEN IMPOSSIBLE to live as we have since 4000 B.C. if Earth had not possessed an abundant supply of iron ore. Prior to that time, nearly all tools and implements had been made of stone or wood. The Neolithic or New Stone Age ended as late as the sixteenth century A.D. in North America, with the development of metallurgy. Most of Earth's supply of extractable iron ore probably came from meteorites. When found in its raw state, these "hard stones" were considered a gift from the gods. Archaeologists speculate that such a stone might have been used in a campfire, where the iron oxides became embedded in the embers, causing the accidental extraction of the common metals. This could be considered the first metallurgical furnace, to which multiple modifications have been made, resulting in what we know today as a blast furnace. The supply of iron ore to Earth from meteorites has dwindled, yet we have dug deeper and deeper to satisfy our dependence on this valuable material.

On a global scale, vast quantities of different metal resources have been found, but they *are* limited. Experts estimate that some of our virgin resources will disappear before the end of the twenty-first century. This deadline is one reason that many countries are working on waste diversion, recycling programs, and a reduction in the use of energy. However, because of the apparently "limitless" supply of resources, we are mining and using these materials at higher rates today—while supposedly being in an energy-conserving mode—than we were when building the infrastructure for many cities and towns across the continent. This mining activity not only depletes the available resources, but also jeopardizes the health of miners and the quality of the environment. Mine tailings may contaminate air, soil, and water for years

*My heart
Is true as steel.*

—WILLIAM
SHAKESPEARE,
*MIDSUMMER NIGHT'S
DREAM*

The Resourceful Renovator

to come, while increased erosion seriously impairs the recovery of impacted areas.

Most metal and ore bodies are located far from their finished product markets. For example, France exports steel frames and concrete panels into Guinea, West Africa, to build structures that require air conditioning and heating systems, support systems that must be imported as well, making the buildings expensive to construct and maintain, and difficult to service. Little spare energy is available to supply air conditioning and elevator service to a region with frequent power outages and water cutoffs. As well, metal does not stand up well in many tropical regions, as the humid, salt sea air can lead to rust and corrosion. Ironically, Guinea has one of the world's richest sources of bauxite, the major aluminum ore, but almost all of the bauxite is shipped out of the country for processing. Sending products to regions that cannot support them is similar to producing materials that our recycling systems cannot process. We need to close the loop on the production, use, and reuse of these materials, while not taxing our existing resources to manufacture, transport, and build them.

FACT

The energy saved by recycling one aluminum can is equivalent to approximately half its volume in gasoline.

—William Rees

VALUE OF METAL BUILDING MATERIALS

The embodied energy in metal products is among the highest of any building materials. While such energy costs may not be reflected in the price of the new material, we pay for this energy one way or another: in higher healthcare costs for metalworkers and for those living in communities where the soil, water, or air have been contaminated by mining or processing, and in deterioration of the environment. Meanwhile, metals are durable substances that can be reused in a variety of ways.

BUILDING MATERIAL	PAID SALVAGE VALUE	PAID (OR CHARGED) TO RECYCLE MATERIAL +/-	NEW MATERIAL PURCHASE PRICE	USED MATERIAL PURCHASE PRICE	DENSITY OF MATERIAL	EMBODIED ENERGY TO CREATE MATERIAL
METAL	$CAD[1]	$CAD/lb.[2]	$CAD[3]	$CAD [4]	lbs./ft.[5]	BTU/lb.
½ inch copper pipe/ft.	0.15	(0.85)	0.51	0.40	0.285–0.344	45,493[8] 1,430 (recycled)[7]
10 inch steel I-beam/ft. (10³/₁₆ x 5³/₄ inches with ³/₄-inch flanges)	3.00–5.00	0.00	0.85–1.10/lb. 15.00–20.00/ft	5.00–10.00	22.000	4,962[6] 2,860 (recycled)[7]
Aluminum storm door (without glass)	5.00	(0.65)	50.00	20.00	165.000 lbs./cu. ft.	8,970[7]
Cast-iron radiator	50.00	0.00	n/a	150.00	450.000 lbs./cu. ft.	6,688[6]
Rebar (½-inch diameter)	n/a	0.00	n/a	n/a	.670	4,300[6]

1 Based on prices from Renovators Resource, Halifax, Nova Scotia, November 1999.

2 Based on prices from John Ross & Sons Ltd., Halifax, Nova Scotia, November 1999.

3 Based on prices from W. A. Moir Metals, Halifax, Nova Scotia, November 1999 (for ¼-inch-thick plate stock).

4 Based on prices from Harbour Metal Recycling Ltd., Dartmouth, Nova Scotia, November 1999 (dependent on season).

5 Based on values from Thomas J. Glover, *Pocket Reference,* 2nd Edition (Littleton, Colo.: Sequoia Publishing, 1995).

6 Canada Mortgage and Housing Corporation, "Optimize," October 1991, p. 5, Table 2.1.

7 Arnold J. Aho, *Materials, Energy and Environmental Design* (New York: Garland STM Press, 1981).

8 George Baird and Michael Donn, *Energy Performance of Buildings* (Boca Raton: CRC Press, 1984).

Cast-iron grate.

The key to using metals in buildings appropriately is in understanding the tremendous amounts of energy and mined materials that are required to make metal. The more recent practice of recycling all types of metal does lower the energy level required. However, in areas where a material isn't a virgin resource, or where a manufacturer or recycling facility doesn't exist, the choice to incorporate metal into buildings on a large scale must be questioned. The intertwined rate of growth of our cities and industries and the depletion of our natural resources requires serious thought about how to sustainably develop the remaining stock of resources. The twenty-first century may well be the last era for the extraction of many minerals that we now think of as abundant and accessible.

FACT

An excavation at L'Anse Aux Meadows, on the northern tip of the Great Northern Peninsula of Newfoundland, shows evidence of ironworking and carpentry. Radiocarbon dating, building types, and artifacts have led researchers to believe that the site was occupied between 990 and 1050 A.D., making it the first known iron smelting location in the New World. It is thought that the smelter was used to produce iron for nails to repair fishing boats. Artifacts such as iron nails and rivets, a lamp, a bronze pin, and sewing tools have been found.

—Priit J. Vesilind, "In Search of Vikings," *National Geographic,* May 2000.

FORGING AHEAD: METALLURGY ANCIENT AND MODERN

The principal metals used in building construction are iron, steel, copper, and aluminum. As well, many alloys, such as brass or bronze, or composite metals, provide a wider variety of metals to build with. Metals have been used in such broad applications as the structural skeleton of a building, electrical distribution conduits, protective coverings and sheathings (such as metal roofing), light fixtures, hardware, and appliances. Metal is one of the most adaptable building materials, due to its malleability when heated, and its stability and strength. It is also one of the most energy-intensive materials to process from its raw state in the ground into finished products.

Iron, specifically, was the most influential metal in developing early civilizations. In these earliest methods for firing iron, smiths forced air into a mixture of iron ore and coke in a furnace. This smelting technology paved the way for the Industrial Revolution, with its enormous demand for casting in the manufacture of machinery, and later for building components such as fences, balconies, and hardware.

A Nova Scotia coal mine in 1880. Coke, one of the main ingredients in iron and steel, is distilled from coal. While coal mining has been made more efficient by mechanization, the process of extracting coal from underground pits or by surface mining remains extremely dangerous and unhealthy for miners, and destructive to the environment.

Underground in coal mine in 1990s.
Iron is produced by combining iron ore, coke, and limestone in a blast furnace. Blasts of air up to 870 degrees Celsius ignite the coke, which melts the iron. The limestone combines with the nonferrous compounds in the ore to form a slag, which rises to the top of the molten iron, and is removed. Slag is generally treated as a waste product and is discarded, though in some regions, slag has found new markets as a cement replacement in concrete. The blast furnace produces what is commonly known as pig iron, the basic ingredient of steel. It requires 2 tons of iron ore, $2/3$ ton of coke, and $1/2$ ton of limestone to make 1 ton of pig iron—the remaining $2\frac{1}{6}$ tons of material is discarded as slag. Pig iron is sometimes used in foundries to make cast items, but is more likely to be used in steel production.

Blacksmith John Little. One of the earliest uses of iron ore was to produce wrought iron. "Wrought" iron is "worked" on the anvil by hammering while it is hot, cooling, or sometimes cold. This ironwork was formed by heating iron ore in charcoal furnaces until it was pasty and then working and purifying it by hammering, but never intentionally melting it. Wrought iron has a fibrous structure, is light gray in color, and when hot can be hammered out, twisted, or stretched. The more it is worked the denser, harder, and more brittle it becomes, but it can be brought back to its original state by reheating it.

Small blacksmith shops still exist across the continent. Small forges are set up to repair and reproduce pieces for many uses. In Nova Scotia, blacksmith John Little has been extending the art of "smithing" to support the local fishing industry.

Wrought iron decorative hinge. Though the majority of his work involves repairing parts for sea-going vessels, the nature of the material with which John Little works is suited to practical and decorative building materials. Little made this hinge to replace a rusted hinge for a heavy wooden door.

Armillary sphere in wheat field in Saskatchewan. John Little is also a well-known metal artist who forges his sculptures, blow-by-blow, into beautiful and functional pieces. This sundial, known as an armillary sphere, was forged in Little's shop.

A building designed by architect
Helmut Jahn in Philadelphia.

METALLURGY ANCIENT AND MODERN

The major raw materials required for the production of steel are pig iron, old steel, limestone, high-quality iron ore, and coke. Smaller quantities of lead and zinc are also used. Even recycling your household tin cans provides some of the feedstock for steel making. This process is energy intensive and involves large-scale equipment. The iron ore is initially crushed and concentrated at the mine, and is then transported to a steel plant in the form of pellets. Limestone is quarried, crushed, and screened before being shipped to the steel plant. After firing in the furnace, the molten steel is poured into ingot molds. Ingots vary in size from 9 to 23 tons and are removed from the molds after cooling. They are then reheated to a temperature high enough to make rolled steel. Ingots are used to produce a variety of construction products including rods, bars, plates, pipe, wire, bolts, nails, sheet steel, and rivets.

Steel can be produced in various grades, depending on where it will be used. Elements such as aluminum, chromium, manganese, and molybdenum, can be added to steel to produce certain characteristics. Steel can provide flexibility in design, while still providing strength and structural stability. It is durable, repairable, reusable, and completely recyclable. Some grades of steel perform well at very high temperatures while others excel in ultra-low temperature situations. Some steels are produced for structural capacity and others for electrical conductivity. Steels can also be made to be electrically resistant. There are rust-resistant steels, impact-resistant steels, and others that take and hold a sharp edge. The steel that we encounter most often on a construction site would be in the form of joists, beams, sheet metal, roofing, siding, decking, framing, and partitions.

Cast-iron grates. Cast iron, produced in China as early as the sixth century A.D., is thought to have been introduced into Great Britain in the fifteenth century from Germany, where the blast furnace made it possible to heat iron hot enough to flow. Cast iron is much different from wrought iron, as it is "cast" in molds and not worked after being poured. The use of cast iron flourished later than wrought iron, mainly from the end of the eighteenth century, though castings were still quite small at that time. Because of its chemical makeup, cast iron resists rust better than steel. This is why it is used inside stoves and furnaces and in a variety of external uses. Its greatest disadvantage is that it is brittle and may crack if dropped or struck with a hammer.

Scrap aluminum awaiting recycling.
Manufacturing aluminum takes a
tremendous amount of energy—about 10
kilowatt-hours (kWh) for each pound of
metal produced. As a result, most
aluminum smelters are located near large,
low-cost power sources, usually
hydroelectric. Aluminum ore (bauxite) is
strip-mined in various parts of the world
and then shipped to smelters. Aluminum is
a lightweight metal (one-third the weight of
copper), but has relatively low strength. It
is corrosion resistant, reflects heat and
light, and is easy to weld. Aluminum also
extrudes well, and as a result is one of the
most versatile construction materials.

Extruded metal materials include door and
window jambs, rails, curtain-wall panel
frames, and mullions. Sheet aluminum,
only a small percentage of which is
recycled, is used for roofing, siding,
flashing, drains, and weather stripping. It is
estimated that 80 percent of the world's
aluminum could be recycled, whereas only
30 percent is being recycled today. More
specifically, only about 15 percent of the
aluminum used in the construction
industry is recovered and recycled. To
preserve this valuable metal, we must find
better ways to reuse and recycle the
aluminum that we are using in our
buildings.

Copper piping. As with other metals, the mining of copper
carries a high environmental price, including toxic gases
released by smelting and leaching of toxins from the slag
heaps left behind. Copper is used for rod, wire, sheet
copper, pipe, tube, and castings. Copper wire is an
excellent electrical conductor and is used in numerous
wiring and electronic applications. It is also well suited to
exterior use because of its color and corrosion resistance.
Initially, copper weathers to a brown color and then takes
on a light green patina, as the surface of the copper
oxidizes. Most people identify copper roofing with this
patina, and paint manufacturers are reproducing this color,
as it is considered an attractive finish.

Brass is the most common of the copper alloys. Brass
is usually a compound of copper and zinc, though other
elements such as lead and tin may be used in the mix.
Normal brass contains 60 to 70 percent copper.

USE

Early forged metal works were for purely functional or practical purposes. Strap hinges, door hardware and knockers, firedogs, cranes, and weathervanes (not to mention horseshoes, harness parts, and other farming implements) made up the inventory of many blacksmith shops.

Cast iron was first used in buildings for aesthetic and economic reasons. Some of the earliest cast-iron implements were firebacks, grave slabs, cannons, cannonballs, and cooking utensils. Most decorative metalwork made today uses derivations of early casting methods. Several of the earliest known pieces of cast iron for structural use in buildings were fashioned in the English Coalbrookdale furnace built in 1638: iron pipes for the palace of Versailles in the 1660s and cast iron columns for a monastery in Portugal in 1752. However, it was probably the famous 100-foot bridge near Coalbrookdale that established cast iron as a structural material in Britain. Iron also became a substitute for timber beams and columns in masonry construction.

Fence patterns. Decorative forms of metalwork, such as balconies, railings, fences, and gates, were developed in the late eighteenth century in North America. To this list can be added brackets, foot scrapers, cornicework, decorative emblems, fountains, and birdbaths.

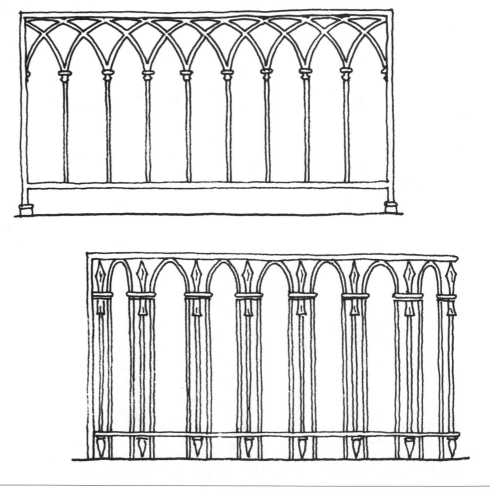

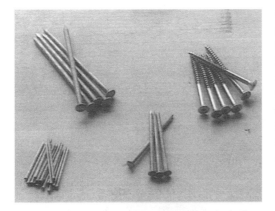

Common, galvanized nails and screws. Most of the smallest elements in construction are made of metal. Fasteners such as nails, bolts, and screws are used in all types of buildings, from residential to industrial. To make dismantling and reusing easier, it is crucial that the type of fastener chosen is one that will not only work for the intended purpose, but also be able to be removed when desired. The preference is using common, galvanized nails and Robertson head screws (a Canadian invention!), eliminating the need for glues and adhesives.

The John Hancock Center, built in 1970 in Chicago. Structural iron and steel took their place in architecture in the nineteenth and twentieth centuries, replacing brick, stone, or wooden members. Because of its compressive strength, cast iron started a revolution in building construction. It made possible many iron-framed warehouses, factories, and stores, leading to steel-skeleton frames and ultimately, the skyscraper. Initially, the replacement of timber by metal extended the life of many buildings. Previously, woodframe buildings, especially in industrial settings, were often completely destroyed by fire. Over time, the elements that were replaced by steel—columns, beams, braces—became larger and stronger and could span wider distances, though still integrating heavy masonry into the surrounding walls.

REUSE

Reusing metal in its existing form is the most energy-efficient method. As we have seen, metals require a great deal of energy to mine, refine, manufacture into finished goods, and transport to markets. With all of the resources already expended on producing steel, copper, and aluminum articles, if we can reuse them in their existing form with little reworking, then we will not consume additional energy and natural resources in remanufacturing.

In many older-home renovations, standard "off-the-shelf" items often do not suit the decor or period of the house. If a salvaged item is not available, you may be lucky enough to find a blacksmith or farrier to build what you need. Reproducing an item in the tradition of the applicable situation continues the appropriate use and reuse of the materials.

Typical demolition of commercial building. Although not considered for this demolition project, steel-framed buildings are more adaptable to dismantling and re-erecting than woodframe structures. Metal buildings often can be dismantled by disconnecting plates and beams joined by bolts or welds. If designed and built to be dismantled, not even a weld need be cut to dismantle the structure. This practice is more frequent within the industrial sector.

Because of their durability, it is worthwhile investing time to salvage steel frames. If properly protected from rust, steel can be used and reused in its existing shape for many years. Lighter frame structures, made from aluminum and used widely in the construction of sunrooms, greenhouses, and entry systems, are also very adaptable to dismantling and reuse. For a great example, read the success story "Greenhouses Get a Second Chance" at the end of this chapter.

RADIATOR REDUX

Salvaged cast-iron radiators. Cast-iron radiators work so well because their heavy construction acts as a heat storage and transfer medium. Hot water flows through the radiator and heats the unit itself, which then radiates the heat into the room (hence its name). More modern versions of hot water radiators, known as baseboard radiators, certainly are easier to install, at less than one-tenth the weight, but they don't have the mass of water and metal to store the heat. Many people say that once you've lived in a house with hot water heat, it is hard to live with any other type of heating system.

Repairing a cast-iron radiator that has a crack or broken seal can be difficult, as not many companies are set up to pressure test the radiators and reseal the joint, or weld the cracks. Check the phone book under "Plumbing/Heating Contractors and Supplies" for a local contact. You may sell your damaged radiators to a metal recycler for a few dollars, or adopt the popular Maritime tradition—use them for boat moorings!

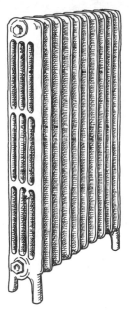

Ornate cast-iron radiators. Certain metal products have great potential to be reused. In cities where hot water heating systems are commonly used, cast-iron radiators are frequently replaced. This type of radiator is not as efficient as more modern, streamlined models, but if only one unit must be replaced, or if you are adding a room to your house and only one additional unit is required, it is much less expensive to reuse an old one than to update the entire heating system.

TRADITIONAL MATERIALS IN NONTRADITIONAL USES

Many metals, such as copper and stainless steel, have been used and reused in a variety of ways. Iron and steel have made a comeback with the sleek, industrial look that is furnishing many interiors and exteriors. The more interesting examples of reuse are usually the ones that use the metal in a situation not originally intended.

Traditional metal grill. This cast-iron grill was made specifically to secure a window opening. The design is very decorative and is more than one hundred years old. This type of custom cast work is still available, though it is very expensive.

Security grill from handrail. An alternative to the old-fashioned security grill is to use a metal handrail. These types of handrails can often be found at used building material stores for less than $20 per 5-foot section. You may wish to enlist the aid of a metalworker to drill and secure the handrail to the window frame.

Bathtub leg wall sconce. The holder for the fixture of this wall sconce is actually an old cast-iron ball-and-claw bathtub leg.

A bathtub leg used as a pattern to cast a second leg to match. Bathtub legs were made in a variety of styles and are actually quite valuable. Some used building material stores may have some in stock, or you can contact a local foundry to reproduce a leg using the sand-cast method.

Residential reuse of metal hospital cabinetry.
Hospital laboratory equipment would not
normally come to mind for homeowners trying
to renovate on a tight budget. Laboratory
equipment and cabinetry is built to extremely
high quality, as the nature of the work requires
the doors and surfaces to be cleaned often and
used frequently. A nice feature that a lot of
institutional cabinetry has is that the cabinets
often have glass doors. The glass doors and the
price attracted homeowner Susan MacKenzie to
use this chrome and glass upper cabinet in her
kitchen. For $75 (CAD), the sliding glass cabinet
door has become a main feature in her kitchen.
When installing an institutional cabinet, ensure
that it can be attached adequately to the
supporting wall. You may have to install wood
blocking between the studs to provide adequate
support for the new/old upper cabinet.

CAST-IRON GRATE TABLE

Large heating grates, along with old
heating systems, are being tossed out, as
new, sleeker heating systems replace the
old ones. Designs on old grates can be
very decorative, as some of the first were
used in the Victorian era, when forced-air
heating systems were being introduced.
This table is of similar construction to
the "Spindle Table with Plank Flooring
Top" in the Wood chapter. Use old spindles, molding, and trim to build the base
of the table. Instead of a solid wood top,
an old cast-iron heating grate makes a
decorative tabletop. Protect with a metal
paint to prevent rusting, for a useful outdoor table or side table.

METAL

TRADITIONAL MATERIALS IN NONTRADITIONAL USES

Rebar door handle by Chris Joyce. Rebar, a steel bar used to reinforce concrete, certainly doesn't have a fine finish to encourage you to consider using it in renovation. Yet artist and sculptor Chris Joyce, of Attica Furnishings in Halifax, Nova Scotia, has used rebar in a number of ways, making wonderful pieces of hardware and furniture.

Copper humidifier. This copper container, now used as a wall hanging, was originally a humidifier. The container would have hung on the edge of a wood-stove or hot water radiator and been filled with water to humidify the air.

Copper pipe wine rack. Copper pipe fetches a relatively high price at metal recyclers, but it also has many potential applications to be reused first. Rob Muise, a talented woodworker, has built many racks and shelving units from salvaged copper pipe of different diameters.

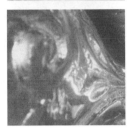

DOORKNOB OR FAUCET COATRACK

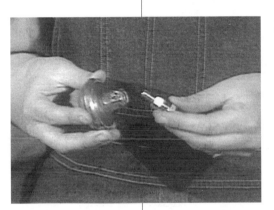

A lot of the fun of working in the salvage business with outdated building materials is in figuring out what else they can be used for. So many items, such as doors and door hardware, windows, and plumbing fixtures, have been replaced by updated systems, resulting in hundreds of thousands of doors, windows, and sinks being thrown out each year. You will see pieces such as this whimsical coatrack in upscale home decorating catalogues, but you can easily make your own from a few discarded faucets and a lintel from an interior door system. A piece of wood planking at least 4 inches wide can be used in place of a lintel.

You can use doorknobs instead of faucets. The key to successfully attaching the hanger to the wood is countersinking a threaded bolt from the rear of the plank to fit snugly to the inner diameter of the faucet or knob. Use a small threaded screw on the faucet or knob to tighten it to the bolt, holding it securely to the wood. Mount the rack to the wall either with screws or by attaching a mounting bracket to the back of the rack.

METAL

SALVAGED FIXTURES AND HARDWARE

Salvaged treasure disguised by many layers of paint. Among the easiest and most sought-after objects to reuse are pieces of old door and window hardware. Early hardware was made from good-quality material (usually solid cast iron, brass, or porcelain), and was designed to suit more elaborate building styles. Many of these pieces are hidden under coats of paint on doors and windows being replaced with newer models.

Hardware cleaned with wire brush and steel wool. A number of reproduction hardware companies specialize in older styles, though most of their wares are made from coated metals. Similar to updating radiators to newer models, reusing old hardware can save time and money. Changing hardware styles from a mortise cartridge to a modern lock requires filling in the cavity with wood and then redrilling a hole to accommodate the new hardware. The cost and embodied energy of comparable new hardware reinforces the case for reusing older styles.

Light restorer's inventory. Reusing metal fixtures is another popular method of recovering metal from old buildings. Early fixtures were designed to hold candles or lard and wicks. Metal provided a fireproof, shiny, reflective surface. Later fixtures were designed for gas. Thin, cast metal pipe was very appropriate for this, as gas does not ignite within sealed metal tubing. Lighting fixtures, especially older models, can be the centerpiece of any renovation. They can be rewired to meet modern standards and electrical codes.

Lighting restoration specialist Brad Haworth. Lighting restoration specialist Brad Haworth has a showroom filled with lighting fixtures from the past. He cleans, repairs, and upgrades fixtures so that they will adorn many more ceiling and walls.

COPPER LIGHT FIXTURE

It is easy to get disenchanted when shopping for new light fixtures . . . not only with the designs, but also with the price! The purpose of a light fixture is twofold: the attraction of the object itself, and the light it radiates to highlight other areas of the room. Very few electrical components are required, and a look at a basic wiring book will show you how to build your own fixture. Basically, if the fixture is properly vented and you use nonflammable materials safely, considering distance from the bulb, it is simple to design your own light. This light fixture was built from scraps of copper tubing, sheet copper, wooden dowel, a new light socket, electrical cord, copper screws, and coated fibrous paper for the screen.

METAL RECYCLING

Most of us are familiar with aluminum and tin can recycling from our household waste stream, but have you ever considered how much recyclable metal is in a typical building? Ferrous metals make up between 5 and 8 percent (by weight) of the construction and demolition (C&D) waste stream. This is a considerable portion of the potential C&D waste stream, though most "waste" metals are already being collected by well-established metal salvage companies. The value of recycled metal depends on its purity, and on the market for the resulting base product. Metal markets can fluctuate daily, sometimes dropping the price paid by half.

Salvageable metals typically include the easily accessible metals that can be stripped from a building. These include copper wiring and piping used for domestic hot water lines, aluminum window and door frames, lighting fixtures and hardware, cast-iron pipe used for hot water heating systems and plumbing, zinc and copper roof flashing, and heating ducts. If removed carefully, many of these materials have the potential to be reused, instead of recycled;

J. Ross and Sons Ltd., typical metal recyclers. Steel is recycled more than any other metal, coming mostly from reinforcing steel, structural steel members, roofing, pipe, tools, nails, screws, hinges, cable, and fencing. Steel can be separated easily from other construction debris with large magnets. Most scrap metal dealers will pick up and occasionally pay for large quantities of scrap metals.

the former requires less energy for production and transportation. An object always has a higher value in its existing state, as it will not require any further energy input to remanufacture it. Nonferrous metals, such as copper, brass, bronze, and aluminum, are even more valuable than steel.

Reusing and recycling of metal construction materials makes perfect sense. The amount of energy saved by reusing or recycling metal is astronomical when all of the mining, manufacturing, and transporting that have been invested in the material are considered. As well, our mines—the dwindling remaining virgin resource—cannot sustain our present levels of industrial growth. Those resources are being depleted without other virgin alternatives. By reusing and recycling this material, we reduce the amount being disposed of in landfills, we preserve the dwindling amount of natural resources, and we save the homeowner and the contractor money by supplying a superior product.

Due to environmental restrictions and performance criteria, many industries, including the steel manufacturing industry, are being required to "clean up their process." Over the past twenty years, steel manufacturers have reduced energy consumption and pollution dramatically, through technological advancement in the manufacturing process. Most steel manufactured today already has a 25 percent recycled content. In fact, manufactured steel requires a recycled proportion to meet quality specifications. So, to a certain extent, this steel already includes earlier mined material, and will be available for reuse for future generations, either reused in its original form, or as a raw material being recycled. Is 25 percent enough? Shouldn't our goal be to exist off the materials already within the loop without mining more? Is this possible?

AMOUNT PAID FOR SALVAGED METALS

METAL	PRICE/LB. ($CAD)[1]
Aluminum, old	0.50
Aluminum, new	0.65
Brass, yellow	0.50
Brass, red	0.60
Cast Iron	0.00
Copper, #1	0.85
Copper, #2	0.70
Sheet Metal	0.00
Stainless Steel	0.22

1 Prices quoted in Halifax, Nova Scotia, December 1999.

The Resourceful Renovator

GREENHOUSES GET A SECOND CHANCE

Four large greenhouses, each approximately 20 by 100 feet, on the grounds of Walter Reed Army Hospital in Washington, D.C., had been scheduled for demolition after the need for these buildings was terminated in 1995. An officer at the hospital, Colonel Martha

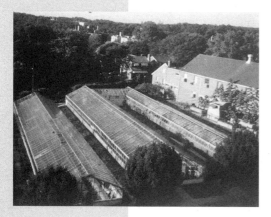

Sanders, pushed for disassembly and reconstruction as an alternative to landfilling these buildings. Representatives from several nearby schools and hospitals looked at the greenhouses, but determined that relocating them would be too costly.

Because the greenhouses were government property, the buildings were subject to projects declared in the McKinley Act, which states that any structural building owned by a government agency or institution that is suitable for habitation should be spared from demolition. Even though the greenhouses did not directly fall under this Act, with its governance, a suitable location for the greenhouses was found nearby at St. Elizabeth's Hospital and the Fort Meade army base.

The potential salvage and disassembly project tempted the Environmental Protection Agency (EPA), National Association of

Greenhouses before, October 14, 1998.
The project seemed huge, as the greenhouses had more than 3,500 panes of glass to carefully dismantle. The greenhouses consisted of concrete foundations and kneewalls, aluminum frames assembled with bolts and screws, and single-paned glass panels approximately 2 feet square. The only tools required to disassemble the frames were wrenches, screwdrivers, and WD-40 to loosen tight connections. The structures were relatively simple in design, without any hidden materials or problems that would make disassembly or resale difficult.

Workers dismantling greenhouse structure.
Many challenges attended this project. An overall disassembly plan was required to respond to the many questions that immediately came from the work crew. Should the project commence from the roof, or should the panels be removed from the ground up? Should all the pieces be completely disassembled, or should some of the frames be left in transportable sections? How should the glass and frames be packed? How should the pieces be labeled so that reassembly would be relatively easy? Many issues were quickly sorted out as work began on the project. One of the first tasks that the trainees were given on-site was to determine which aluminum components were load-bearing and which non-load-bearing. This would make the planning for the disassembly of the structure much easier.

Preparing glass panels for transport. Minimal damage or loss of material was very important, since reassembly would require all of the components to arrive in reusable shape. The glass panels were packed in wooden crates large enough to contain twelve pieces of glass, which were light enough for one person to lift.

Home Builders (NAHB) Research Center, officials at the hospital, and a job training program manager to take on the challenge of saving the material from going to a landfill, while assisting the region in job training. The EPA was instrumental in coordinating the project in the development phase. The NAHB Research Center role was to provide technical assistance to the deconstruction crew. The project was delayed for a period of time while a suitable location for reassembly was found, but in October 1998 the disassembly got underway.

Due to the ease of disassembly and the repetitive nature of the work, this project was well suited to a cooperative job training program. Although the greenhouses were not of woodframe construction, the buildings had analogous components and required similar structural considerations. The on-site training program was accompanied by a ten-week skill development classroom course that included blueprint reading, trade practices and methods, and tool use. The training also involved the use of power tools, which would be common in more conventional construction projects.

Dismantling nearly complete. This project was successful on many accounts. Not only were eighteen people trained on-site, but the greenhouses were salvaged from disposal, and excellent safety practices were employed with only a few minor cuts reported. The result was that only 5 percent of the glass panels broke, and the job was completed one month ahead of schedule.

> **National Association of Home Builders Research Center (NAHB)**
> 400 Prince George's Boulevard
> Upper Marlboro, Maryland 20774-8731
> Toll-Free: 1 (800) 638-8556
> Web site: www.nahbrc.org

Marble quarry face. Slabs of rose- and cream-colored marble are mined from this quarry face in Italy.

Samples of various stone tile finishes and textures.

STONE

THE ORIGIN OF STONE as a building material is much more direct than that of metal, glass, brick, ceramics, or even wood. Stone changes minimally from its point of extraction from the ground to becoming the foundation for a building or the polished countertop in a renovation. On the other hand, some types of stone are found only in remote mountainous regions, or buried deep in the earth. Quarrying this extremely dense and heavy material can be exorbitantly expensive in human labor and machinery. Even these costs are outweighed by the cost to transport the stone, often continents away.

Building stone is found in many regions around the globe and can be mined from a variety of sources in a variety of ways. Glacial deposits became some of the first building stone. In the northeastern United States, a former glaciated area, the first deposits used for construction were the many irregularly rounded stones, known as fieldstones, found directly on the ground. Because they had been shaped by the forces of nature, often with smooth edges, and were a manageable size, they were the easiest stones to collect. Stone that has eroded away from mountains has been a convenient source of building material for centuries. Outcrops or ledges, which are also susceptible to erosion, are another source of building material. Because it was easily accessible, builders frequently used stone from these outcrops, even though this exposed material was generally of low quality.

In earlier days, large stones were often transported on oxen-powered carts. Winter was the best season for this task, because the animals were not needed for farmwork and the ground was firm enough to support a heavy cargo. Quarries on or near navigable water enjoyed the advantage of being able to ship the stone

Never tell me that not one star of all That slip from heaven at night and softly fall Has been picked up with stones to build a wall.

—ROBERT FROST, "A STAR IN A STONEBOAT"

For water continually dropping will wear hard rocks hollow.

—PLUTARCH, A.D. 46–120

A coursed ashlar stone face in excellent condition.

considerably longer distances by barge, raft or boat. On land, stone was transported by horse and wagon, rail, and later, transport trucks.

High-quality stone, such as marble for trim and ornamental building components, has a high value in proportion to its weight, and is often shipped considerable distances. The manufacture of these specialty items expanded into a major industry, concentrated in selected cities where skilled artisans came to work the stone. Stonecutters face hazards in their workplace, including lung disease

A poorly maintained coursed ashlar stone face with deteriorating concrete jointwork.

from the stone dust and injuries from cutting tools. As a general rule, importing large amounts of stone is prohibitively expensive, but it is still an active industry for high-end renovations and construction. Factories continue to produce funerary monuments, as well as building components. Obviously, the reuse of these durable and valuable materials makes more sense than continuing to extract, manufacture, and transport new stone products.

VALUE OF STONE BUILDING MATERIALS

As shown in the last column of this chart, the embodied energy of most stone products is relatively small compared to other building materials, because stone often can be used with minimal processing. Transportation, the costs of which have not been included here because they can vary so widely, of course requires fossil fuel, with an accompanying environmental penalty.

Gypsum wallboard, also called drywall or "Sheetrock," is composed of a core of gypsum covered on each side with paper. While this is one of the simplest and least expensive wall surfaces to install, taping the joints between pieces prior to painting can be time consuming. Some gypsum board recycling facilities are now operating to alleviate the environmental burden at landfill sites.

BUILDING MATERIAL	PAID SALVAGE VALUE	PAID (OR CHARGED) TO RECYCLE MATERIAL +/-	NEW MATERIAL PURCHASE PRICE	USED MATERIAL PURCHASE PRICE	DENSITY OF MATERIAL[3]	EMBODIED ENERGY TO CREATE MATERIAL
STONE	$CAD	$CAD/cu.ft.[1]	$CAD[2]	$CAD[6]	lbs./cu. ft.	BTU/lb.
Granite foundation stone (12" x 18" x 36")	10.00–20.00	0.00	100.00–300.00	75.00	168.0	88[4]
Slate flooring tile (12" x 12" x 1/4" thick)	0.50	0.00	10.00–15.00	5.00–8.00	168.0	88[4]
Marble flooring tile (12" x 12" x 3/4" thick)	0.50	0.00	25.00–40.00	10.00–18.00	160.0	88[4]
Gypsum board (1/2" x 48" x 96")	0.00	(0.02)	10.00	5.00	52.8	2,600[5]

1 Based on prices from Halifax Construction & Debris Recycling Ltd., Halifax, Nova Scotia, November 1999.

2 Based on prices from Nova Tile and Marble, Ltd., Dartmouth, Nova Scotia, November 1999.

3 Based on values from Thomas J. Glover, Pocket Ref, 2nd Edition (Littleton, Colo.: Sequoia Publishing, 1995).

4 Canada Mortgage and Housing Corporation, "Optimize," October 1991, p. 5, Table 2.1.

5 Center for Renewable Energy and Sustainable Technology (CREST) Web site: www.solstice.crest.org.

6 Based on prices from Renovators Resource, Inc., Halifax, Nova Scotia, November, 1999.

MINING AND
PROCESSING STONE

Quarry operation in Wallace, Nova Scotia, c. 1885. Most methods of quarrying stone are more involved than simply collecting field stones from the surface. A fully commercial quarry has a large source of stone, whether readily accessible ten feet down or hundreds of feet below the surface of the earth. This photo depicts quarrying at the turn of the century, using derricks to hoist the large sandstone blocks to the surface.

Quarrying landscaping pavers. Modern quarries may not appear very different from those from one hundred years ago. This quarry, near Verona, Italy, provides landscaping pavers, which have been cut and loaded onto a cart. This same marble, called Brecchia Damascata, is shown in some interior finish photos later in this chapter.

Wet saw cutting granite. Water is used to cool and lubricate the sawblade as it cuts through granite. Stonecutters must wear a respirator and eye protection against the hazardous stone dust created by this process.

Worker edge-polishing granite. Hundreds of diamond chips glued to a plastic base form the grinding surface of the machine used to give stone a smooth finish. These diamond chips are prohibitively expensive.

STONE
USE

Stone has been used for centuries as a building material for the crudest and the finest buildings. It endures where other building materials do not. The fact that historians can study the methods of construction of stone structures thousands of years old still standing today is a testament to their durability.

Until the fifteenth century A.D., cut stones were used primarily for the construction of roads, bridges, viaducts, and castles. We are witnesses to this work, as remnants of Roman buildings, roads, and aqueducts still exist. To this day, stone buildings exude an air of wealth and status. Though many cultures in the world utilized stone construction, few North American historic buildings were

Anasazi dwellings in Mesa Verde. The stone housing of the Anasazi Indians in the southwestern United States, inhabited from about A.D. 400 to 1200, is an example of early North American natural stone dwellings. This resourceful siting in a naturally occurring outcrop, preserved in Mesa Verde National Park, shows a complex arrangement of homes, storage buildings, and public spaces. Evidence from over thousands of years shows that humans lived in natural rock shelters throughout the world, from the caves of the Henan province in northeastern China to the remote mountain regions of Spain and Tunisia.

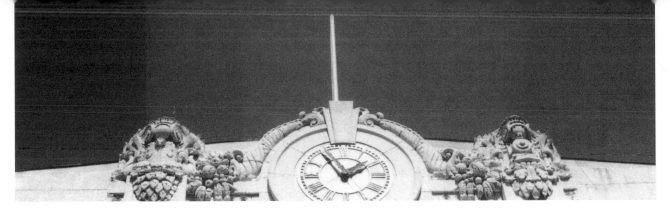

Carved stone parapet, Canadian Pacific Railway Building, Winnipeg, Manitoba.

built of this material. The first stone buildings were quite simple in design. As the use of stone increased, so did the elaborateness of the design, often incorporating arches and vaults. Only the most expensive structures were elaborately finished in early times, but as more people prospered, demand grew for marble chimney pieces, stone steps, and sills. Even simple buildings had stone foundations and sometimes stone chimneys; however, this material was only roughly finished.

Stone is generally brittle, though it is surprising to note the difference between a soft slate and a hard granite. In general, stone can sustain heavy, compressive loads better than the stress of bending. It is most effectively used in walls and piers but can also be used in beams of limited span. Because of its immense weight and the difficulty of transporting stone from a quarry to a home, few people have a choice of what kind of stone to use. This choice is dependent on the decision of the quarry operators, the market profits, and the transporter. In areas where good building stone was found, stone construction flourished.

FACT

Maybe not quite a home, at least for the living, the Chephron Pyramid in Giza, Egypt, was built around 2650 B.C. According to Herodotus, it took 100,000 men twenty years to build this structure. These monuments were built without the machinery that we would now require to rebuild the very same structure. The sheer ingenuity required to complete these buildings still puzzles researchers today.

One of earliest stone houses east of Quebec. New immigrants to North America arriving in the late 1600s, familiar with stone and rubble construction, built many stone buildings. The Dutch, Scots, Swiss, Germans, and French all continued to use their skills in building with what was around them—stone. This stone house in Newport Landing, Nova Scotia, is thought to be one of the oldest stone houses in Canada, east of Quebec. It has intricate brick archwork in the basement, and impressive stone walls.

STONE

TYPES, ORIGINS, AND USES OF STONE

Different types of stone are formed in different ways, and are composed of various aggregates of minerals. Formation and composition both affect the hardness, crystal structure, cleavage, color, susceptibility to weathering, and other qualities of the material.

IGNEOUS
Igneous rock is formed by the solidification of lava or magma, usually from volcanic activity.

TYPE	CHARACTERISTICS	COLOR	USES
Granite	A coarse-grained rock comprised of quartz, mica, and feldspar. Crystalline, granular, hard, strong, durable, and impervious to water.	Varies in color from white to silver gray, sometimes with red or pink throughout.	Widely used as building material, including for foundations, paving and curbstones, steps.
Basalt	Formed by volcanic activity. Found mainly in Scotland.	Durable gray stone that weathers to a smooth blue.	Paving material.
Serpentine	Comprised mainly of magnesium silicate. Has a fine grain, homogeneous structure, and no cleavage planes.	Olive green to greenish black. Impurities may add other colors.	Wainscoting, windowsills, stair treads, and landings. Verde antique is especially valued as elegant veneer paneling.

SEDIMENTARY
Sedimentary rocks are formed from mineral particles deposited by water, and become available as a building material as igneous rocks erode, exposing the underlying rock.

TYPE	CHARACTERISTICS	COLOR	USES
Sandstone	Formed from particles deposited in ancient river beds. Comprised mainly of quartz grains set in a matrix of silt, clay, silica, or carbonate cement.	Wide range of colors, grain size, and textures.	Used for ashlar veneer and rubble walls.
Limestone	Formed from particles deposited on ancient ocean floors. Comprised of calcium and magnesium carbonates with silica, and aluminum and iron oxides.	Varies in color from gray blue to creamy white.	Most common building stone. Used for paneling, ashlar veneer, windowsills, copings, facings, flagstone, hearths, mantels, and sculpture.
Shale	Composed of mud and clay. Generally thought of as a poorer quality building material.	Reddish brown to black.	Used in rubble walls, or as backup stone behind stone walls.
Gypsum	A soft, powdery, nearly pure mineral rock, formed as a chemical precipitate from the evaporation of saline lakes or seas.	White, or delicately colored in shades of yellow or light red.	Alabastar, a fine-grained massive, is used for statuary and ornamental trim. The crude form is valuable for plasters, cements, wallboard, and tile and block products.

METAMORPHIC
Metamorphic rocks are created when either igneous or sedimentary rocks are subjected to enormous heat and pressure deep within Earth's crust.

TYPE	CHARACTERISTICS	COLOR	USES
Slate	Fine-grained metamorphic equivalent of shale that is easier to cut than most other rock; can also be split easily along natural planes.	Comes in a variety of generally dark colors, including gray, black, green, purple, red, and mottled.	Roofing, floor and wall tile, flagging, dimension stone, blackboards, billiard table bases. In crushed form, for roofing tile aggregate, other applications.
Marble	Metamorphosed limestone or dolostone. Can be polished and carved with relative ease. However, due to its softer qualities, it is susceptible to weathering, and will lose its luster if exposed to the elements.	One of the most colorful of all building stones. Ranges from pure white to black, violet, red, yellow, pink, and green, with a variety of veining and patterns.	Extensively used for facades, flooring, steps, sidewalks, gravestones, statuary, mantels, sills and benches.
Alabaster	A rarer rock, too soft to be exposed on exterior facades on buildings.	Creamy white color with veins of pink.	Used for interior decorative purposes.
Mica	Cleaves easily into thin, shiny sheets. Tolerates high temperature without deformation.	Brown, black, or white; nearly transparent in thinnest sheets.	Once used for windowpanes, especially in stoves or furnaces.

Marble hallway. A marble floor of many-colored tiles exudes sheer elegance, but is also exceptionally durable and easy to clean.

Kitchen countertop made from Quebec granite. Granite is widely used for countertops, as seen in this contemporary kitchen. This granite, called Rose Riviere, is from northern Quebec.

Marble table and fireplace. Although stone is often used as an exterior building material, it should also be considered for interior furnishings. This fireplace and table were built from Brecchia Damascata marble from the quarry near Verona, Italy, shown earlier. The name means "broken silk" in Italian, describing the colorful fractured surface and veining of the stone.

STONE
REUSE

Stone storage yard at marble and tile company. Frequently, you can obtain scrap pieces of interesting stone from marble and tile companies. Since this material usually represents a disposal cost, most companies will allow customers to remove any offcuts, free of charge, ready to make a new creation from a traditional waste material.

Stone may be one of the more challenging materials to reuse, because of its sheer weight. For many reasons, stone or brick structures are difficult, but not impossible, to move. The mortar often fails with any movement or stress, though by numbering the pieces and careful documentation, many stone buildings have re-emerged in new locations.

However, because such a great deal of energy has already been expended to fabricate it into a building material, stone should be reused wherever possible. One potential concern with reusing stone is the added work required if it must be reworked to a different size. This involves special tools and skills, normally out of reach of most homeowners and contractors. If you are considering reusing some type of stone or block in your renovation, try to measure and inspect it prior to making final design decisions. Using the material with its existing dimensions eliminates the recutting expenses, and will achieve the highest end use for the stone. This will also preclude the requirement to remove any further raw material from our ecosystem. If a few cuts are required, contact a stone or masonry company, which should have the necessary stone-cutting equipment available.

Salvage yards and demolition sites are potential sources of stone to reuse in your renovation. However, most demolition companies will not take the time to remove stonework, as it is time consuming to loosen from the mortar, heavy to remove, and costly to transport and store. A person with proper liability insurance to cover access to construction sites could probably salvage many pieces. Heavy equipment is often required to retrieve granite foundation stones, columns, pillars, pediments, large windowsills, and door lintels. When recovering larger stone blocks, consult with the demolition contractor to coordinate work with a heavy equipment operator.

Around the turn of the century, institutional buildings such as hospitals and schools were built predominately of brick or stone. Even the windowsills, stair treads, and door thresholds were often made of marble or granite. Today, this type of building is being replaced by more versatile, energy-efficient buildings and many of the original buildings are being demolished and landfilled. Salvaging their stone components will often result in high-value material with a lot of history.

Scrap granite slabs. Quarries, monument shops, salvage yards, and even demolition sites may have scrap heaps of cut or polished stone in pieces that are manageable but still large enough to make useful and beautiful furnishings in your home.

STONE
ON FIRM FOOTING

One component of a late nineteenth- and early twentieth-century institutional building that can be particularly valuable to recover from a demolition is the foundation. Such structures were frequently built on slabs of solid granite, which will likely be as sturdy today as when they were laid one hundred years ago. Since builders often used no mortar, these foundation stones are relatively easy to recover and reuse, especially if you can find a new role for them that does not require recutting.

Granite foundation blocks. These granite foundation stones were salvaged from an old school that was demolished a few years ago.

A salvaged church . . . The granite has been reused as foundation stone for this beautiful church, which was also salvaged from the wrecking ball and moved to a pristine site. The granite blocks were measured and recorded individually. The overall size of the church, and its footprint on the site, were designed using the entire stone block, and very little had to be reworked in the final design.

. . . rises again. Granite certainly gives this building a solid, secure, and beautiful base for the century-old board-and-batten Gothic church to rise above.

PUTTING THE PIECES TOGETHER

The photographs on these pages demonstrate that the Resourceful Renovator isn't limited to working with any single reused building material. Here are ideas for every room in the house—and beyond.

Salvaged granite foundation blocks provide solid front steps. See "Stone," page 79.

A few discarded faucets and a door lintel form this amusing coat rack. See "Metal," page 58.

Dovetailed joints make any reclaimed wood project look classy.

A multipane storm window may no longer serve well in an exterior function, but graces an entry hall with a mirror. See "Glass," page 123.

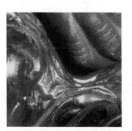

A salvaged wood cornice bracket and a marble tile from the floor of a hospital demolition make a decorative shelf. See "Stone," page 87.

Salvaged brick serves as an elegant and multifunctional fireback for this classic enameled cast-iron woodstove. See "Brick," page 109.

A storm window, hinged to open, brings light and air into an interior dining room. See "Glass," page 125.

A plain old single-pane window, some bits of molding and wainscoting or wood paneling, salvaged butt hinges, and a window lock—an "antique" jelly cabinet. See "Glass," page 127.

Salvaged glass blocks and light fixtures add a quaint—yet functional—touch to a new café. See "Glass," page 130.

Copper pipe, lath, and some short, sturdy planking make a fine wine rack. See "Metal," page 59.

A hefty slab of Carrera marble salvaged from a commercial building and the indestructible cast-iron legs of an old school desk are joined in this sturdy side table. See "Stone," page 87.

A recut 1880s marbleized slate mantel and soapstone hearth make this new Bellfire fireplace feel at home with the softwood floors and plaster walls of this century-old house. See "Stone," page 85.

Salvaged plank flooring and reclaimed hand-hewn beams add character to a new home. See "Wood," page 28.

Salvaged thermopane windows foster houseplants in this sunroom converted from a tiny pantry kitchen. See "Glass," page 125.

Salvaged wooden spindles form legs, wood molding and plywood form the table base, and reused ceramic tiles form the top of this table. See "Ceramics," page 146.

Wooden molding and flooring find many ingenious uses, such as this clever clock.

Porch columns frame the bed in this innovative renovation. The headboard is made from a five-panel wooden door. See "Wood," page 31.

Softwood flooring forms this simple end table.

Scrap copper tubing and sheet copper shine in this coated-paper light fixture. See "Metal," page 61.

Old wooden doors and cast-iron hinges find new life in this nine-drawer chest. See "Wood," page 30.

Street-paving bricks are durable enough for a garden path in any climate. See "Brick," page 107.

Fieldstone walls and monuments grace Standing Stone Perennial Farm. See "Stone," page 79.

Bricks from the old front porch at his parents' house found a new role in this builder's barbeque. See "Brick," page 109.

Stone monuments are not just ancient history. The owners of the Standing Stones Perennial Farm, in Royalton, Vermont, find large chunks of schist when they till the fields. Instead of dragging them away, they erect the boulders to grace the gardens and paths. You can learn how to build your own stone circles or monuments in Rob Roy's *Stone Circles: A Modern Builder's Guide to the Megalithic Revival.*

STAIR TREAD AND BOULDER GARDEN BENCH

The most important preparation for a stone garden bench is a proper foundation. A resourceful foundation technique is to dig two trenches 2 feet deep and 3 feet apart (from center to center). Fill the trenches with gravel, and tamp to a level grade. Set the base rocks (approximately 20 to 24 inches tall) in place, ensuring stable support for the bench. With a level, adjust the rocks with gravel to make each support equal in height. Place a granite stair tread or stone slab that is a minimum of 2 inches thick by 5 feet long by 1 foot wide across the supports. Use small stones to shim the slab, to minimize any movement of the bench.

Granite blocks used as front steps. Salvaged granite blocks have become the perfect front steps for this new home built in the Nantucket style. The blocks were carefully chosen from a pile of foundation blocks that were stored in a contractor's yard. The two blocks make a perfect set of front steps. A boom truck was required to hoist the blocks into position. The blocks have been laid upon two concrete support piers that come out from the foundation wall, just beneath grade, at a 90 degree angle. Pouring two concrete piles below the frost line would also be adequate to ensure that the granite blocks don't heave and shift when the ground freezes and thaws.

PAVING THE WAY

Basalt pavers used in driveway. Many old city streets were paved with basalt paving stones, known as blue stones, or cobblestones. With repeated repairing and repaving of these streets, occasionally the original road base is removed to create enough depth for new road material. Blue stones, which come from the Irish Sea coastline of Scotland, are highly sought after to add beauty to exterior and interior environments. The stone's magnificent blue color is produced by repeated surface wear, such as by horse and buggy or car traffic.

Fieldstone patio. Fieldstones are a perfect landscaping material when used to edge gardens and create pathways. Alexander Johnston, an acupuncturist and doctor of Chinese medicine, installed this patio and garden behind his lovely Georgian farmhouse, which he is restoring as Freegrace Commons, a coalition of complementary health professionals in Quechee, Vermont.

Other paving cobbles are round, smooth beach stones or flat fieldstones, which were brought to the towns and villages to pave the roads. These stones were placed on edge, stone-to-stone, to create a solid surface away from mud and puddles.

BLUE STONE PATH

After years of traffic, the surface of old basalt paving stones become smooth in texture and take on a beautiful blue hue. Many basalt streets have been excavated to lay improved infrastructure during resurfacing and repaving. These stones can find a perfect home as a pathway or patio.

Blue stones.

My business partner, Susan Helliwell, created a wonderful path connecting her driveway to the back porch. She notes that "once the design is figured out, the project is a lot of fun."

Laying a blue stone path doesn't require many tools. You will need landscaping fabric, sand, and a bed of gravel for a proper base for the path. A shovel, edger, and rake help to create the line to be paved and to make a level surface. Use string and wooden markers to lay out the blue stone area. After you have all the necessary items, dig down 7 to 8 inches, and remove grass and dirt to reuse elsewhere. Edge the area with a straight-bladed shovel. Rake the surface even. Lay landscaping fabric on the raked surface with adequate material to cover the sides of stones at the perimeter line. Lay gravel 3 inches deep, and tamp it down with the shovel. Spread 1 inch of sand over the gravel, and tamp. Start laying the blue stone in your chosen pattern. Paths work best when the stone is laid in an overlapping pattern, similar to brick or tilework. To ensure a tight fit, clean surplus material from the edges of the stones with a mason's hammer, and lightly tap each stone into place with a rubber mallet. Once the area is covered, spread sand over the entire surface, and use a broom to push sand into the cracks between the stones. You may have to do this two or three times, until all cracks have been filled with sand.

FACT

Basalt, formed by volcanic activity, and found in octagonal pillars, was used as ballast on wooden sailing ships. "Ballast," as noted in the *Oxford English Dictionary,* first appeared in written form in 1530. The first known ship to sail from Europe to North America using ballast was the Mayflower in 1620. Basalt stones were used as ballast into the twentieth century.

Walkway of blue stones.

STONE WALLS

Rubble wall in Yorkshire Dales, Great Britain.

Most stone walls and houses that we are familiar with today were built in patterns that fall into one of the following categories:

Uncoursed Rubble Stone: Includes common fieldstones, which are sometimes roughly dressed;

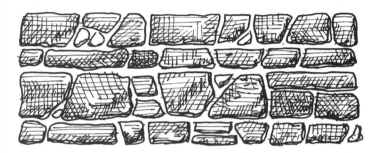

Coursed Rubble Stone: Built of fieldstones in a more uniform pattern;

Broken Ashlar: Outside facing stone is cut, but stone is laid without continuous horizontal joints as in a coursed ashlar;

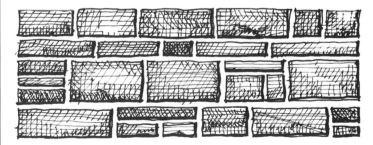

Coursed Ashlar: Uniform stonework, similar to large brickwork, built with cut, not roughly dressed, outside facing stone.

DRY-STONE GARDEN WALL

A dry-stone wall is built without mortar. It takes a lot of practice to perfect the technique, but a dry-stone wall will add quality and character to your landscaping project, if you take the time to do it right.

The best stone for building your own garden wall is either limestone, basalt, or granite. Each piece should have at least one smooth vertical face positioned on the outer surface of the wall. Dig the trench down to the frost line for your area. Lay drainage tile at the perimeter of the trench to ensure proper drainage away from the wall, so water will not undermine the foundation. Use smaller diameter stone rubble (4 to 6 inches) for infill, and gravel to fill the trench.

The tools required are a string to provide a line for the face of the wall, a level to ensure that the wall is vertical, and a hammer to reshape the stones and tap them into place. Start by positioning the largest available pieces of stone to cover the rubble trench, overlapping it by 3 inches. Build the wall a minimum of 18 inches wide.

Continue by placing one layer of stone around the perimeter of the wall. Reserve any stones that have a good 90-degree angle to use as corner stones. Lay all stones as tightly as possible and fill in cavities with small stones. Pack the stones tightly, not coming above the surface of the perimeter stone. Continue stacking perimeter stone, keeping the vertical face as flush as possible with the stone beneath. Make sure to overlap stone joints below with new

First course of laying stone.

stone, similar to brick masonry. When your wall is at the desired height, place large flat stones as a top cap. An option is to finish the top of the wall with a concrete cap. This requires wooden formwork to edge the wall so that the cap will completely cover the stone below. Consult a stonework contractor if you would like a concrete cap.

A CLEAN SLATE

The indelible slate roof. Compared to most marbles, slate is a simple, elegant stone that can have either a polished or rough finish. It tends to have a green, gray, or rose-colored face and is usually consistent in its coloring. Slate can be used as a structural and decorative component of nearly every part of a building. Joe Jenkins celebrates the longevity and durability of slate roofs in his book, *The Slate Roof Bible.* His own house is roofed with recycled slates.

Recycled slate interior paneling. Walls made from slate are unusual in North America, but were widely used in Great Britain. These interior walls in Joe Jenkins house are also recycled slate.

Slate mantel c. 1880 with new Bellfire fireplace. This mantel blends well within this century-old home, though in fact it was just recently added, when the Bellfire open-hearth fireplace was built. The pieces of the mantel were purchased at a used building material store and resized to fit the opening of the fireplace. The shaped top piece, an ogee curve typically used in woodworking, also needed to be recut. The $75 (CAD) per hour cost to recut the slate was minimal, compared to the price of purchasing a new slate mantel. Marbleizing slate, where marble patterns were painted onto a simple slate mantel, was a practice commonly used near the end of the nineteenth century, to add a relatively cheap decoration to the mantel.

INSTALLING A SLATE FLOOR

Rob and Jaki Roy, of the Earthwood Building School in West Chazy, New York, installed a handsome floor in their guest house using recycled roof slates. The Roys poured a concrete slab, applied a bonding compound to the weathered side of the slates, and set the slates in place while the concrete was still plastic. They used a borrowed slate cutter to cut round pieces from some of the more damaged slates.

Jaki, Rob, and their son Rohan pointed the slate floor carefully to be sure to leave no sharp slate edges exposed. Setting eighty slates took about half an hour, and the pointing another hour and a half.

The elegant slate floor was very inexpensive to install, and is easily maintained with the application of a slate floor sealer every year or so.

STONE

INTERIOR FINISHINGS
AND FURNISHINGS

Stored slabs of Carrera marble. Carrera, Italy, is world renowned for its marble, which is shipped around the world for a variety of uses. The white base color, with subtle gray veining, makes it a very attractive and opulent material. Many commercial banking buildings use marble to accentuate the quality and permanence of their institutions. Marble is often used in entrances, foyers, lobbies, boardrooms, bathrooms, and offices. Marble is sometimes used in kitchens, as it is one of the best surfaces for preparing baking dough. However, it is difficult for marble to compete with other materials as countertops, due to the costs of quarrying, transporting, cutting, and custom finishing.

Salvaged Carrera marble table. The owners of a commercial building in downtown Halifax, Nova Scotia, planned to surface the exterior colonnade near the entrance with large slabs of Carrera marble. The marble was improperly installed, and the structural support system failed. The owners replaced the marble with another material. The quality of the Carrera marble exceeded what most stone and tile companies receive from Italy. A tile company purchased the marble and is now installing it in a variety of locations. This side table was made from one of the pieces of the salvaged Carrera marble. The table was built using the cast-iron legs from an old school desk. The legs are mounted to a piece of planking, which is then drilled and mounted on the scrap marble.

Stone radiator cover works well as shelf. Smaller pieces of scrap stone can be used in a variety of situations in the home. Even narrow strips and leftover pieces work well. The stone on this hot water radiator is a perfect material to store heat without being damaged. (Wood may tend to crack or warp with the heat.)

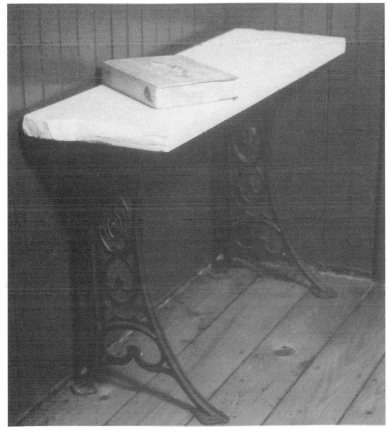

Bracket top made with salvaged marble tile. This decorative bracket is made from salvaged lumber. The 12-inch-square piece of marble was salvaged from the floor of a demolished hospital.

RECYCLING

Compared to the current volumes of wood and metal recycling, little stone from the construction industry is recycled. Stone and rubble from older foundations is being used as clean fill (for land grading and foundations) in new construction.

In regions where stone quarries are well developed and the new aggregate price is relatively cheap, it is currently too expensive to recycle aggregate, other than to use it as clean fill. Until the pricing of building materials correctly reflects all of the life-cycle costs of extracting, manufacture, transportation, and disposal, some recycling opportunities will be left woefully far behind.

One of the bigger advances in construction debris recovery is the recycling of concrete. Concrete, comprised of gravel, sand, cement, and water, can be crushed or pulverized into various-sized aggregates for use in many types of construction projects. Where virgin aggregate is not readily available, and the price for

Recycling equipment at a Florida C&D recycling facility. Because virgin aggregate must be shipped in from other states and available disposal sites are at a premium, the state of Florida serves as a good example in recycling large volumes of concrete.

Recycled aggregate. Many regions are using crushed concrete in the mixture for new concrete. This material can also be used in combination with recycled asphalt shingles as a road base, in areas that are not subjected to an active freeze-thaw cycle.

sand, gravel, and cement are at a premium, recycling concrete makes both economic and environmental sense.

In Germany—where most buildings have been constructed from stone or concrete for some time—the state of recycling aggregates is very advanced. Concrete recycling, more specifically, has been a viable industry for over a decade, with ready markets for the crushed product. A number of factors contribute to the success of aggregate recycling in Germany. First, wood frame construction is not as widely used as it is here in North America; wood is mainly utilized as an interior finish or in roof framing. Second, concrete recycling makes economic sense as Germany's primary resources are minimal, compared to the growth of the country and the need for construction materials. Finally, it is federally legislated that all aggregates must be recycled. With these high standards of recycling for all materials, including packaging, metal, glass, and concrete, Germany has established itself as a leader in the industry.

FACT

The energy required to manufacture the cement portion of concrete far outweighs the total of the other elements. Cement is composed primarily of lime, silica, alumina, iron oxide, and gypsum. The raw materials must first be crushed and blended, then the mixture is burned at 1,300 to 1,500 degrees Celsius (about 2,400 to 2,700 degrees Fahrenheit). Finally, the resulting clinker is ground to a fine powder. Some waste by-products of other industrial processes, such as blast-furnace slag or fly ash from coal-generated power plants, may be used in the manufacture of cement or substituted for part of the cement in concrete, apparently producing a superior product.

A SUCCESSFUL C&D WASTE RECOVERY NETWORK

ReFurnishings.
Even though a complete disassembly salvages most of the material and is the best scenario possible for a salvageable building, some material always remains that does not sell easily. Renovators Resource designs and builds furniture pieces from this supply. Called "ReFurnishings," these pieces use materials such as short spindles, old glass, and wide plank boards in the creation of armoires, tables, bookcases, shelves, and many other items.

Very little was known about construction and demolition (C&D) waste in Nova Scotia before 1994, when the Sustainable Economic Development Agency sponsored two projects to identify and quantify the various broad C&D categories. Two facilities in the Halifax Regional Municipality have been working since then to establish a C&D waste recovery system and to assist the region with its goal of a 50 percent solid waste diversion by the year 2000. The Renovators Resource Inc. is a used building material store, and the Halifax County Construction and Debris Recycling Limited (HCCDRL) is a C&D recycling facility. The two companies were set up independently, but immediately became allies with the common goal of reusing and recycling as much C&D material as possible.

After Renovators Resource recovers all components from a renovation or demolition that are saleable or useful for the production of furniture, some construction material still remains that has little or no reuse potential. This is where the ally company, HCCDRL plays a crucial role in closing the loop. HCCDRL is the only

Renovators Resource Inc.
P.O. Box 36032
Halifax, Nova Scotia
Canada B3J 3S9
Phone: (902) 429-3889
E-mail: frontdesk@renovators-resource.com
Web site: www.renovators-resource.com

Halifax County Construction and Debris Recycling Limited (HCCDRL)
16 Mills Drive
Goodwood, Nova Scotia
Canada B3T 1P3
Phone: (902) 876-8644
Fax: (902) 876-1878

full-spectrum C&D waste recycling facility in eastern Canada that processes any C&D waste material that is not suitable for reuse at Renovators Resource, such as concrete, asphalt, drywall, wood, metal, and brick.

HCCDRL established their C&D recycling facility on a two-acre site on the outskirts of Halifax, Nova Scotia, in May 1995. The initial plan was to receive and process clean wood and asphalt shingles into usable products. The company started out with three employees and an old Pettibone "Payloader." During the first six months of operation, HCCDRL processed approximately 3,500 metric tonnes of material. Today, HCCDRL has almost $3 million (CAD) worth of loading and processing equipment, employs twenty to thirty people full-time, and processes 15,000 tonnes of C&D waste per year. At present, HCCDRL recycles more than 95 percent of the redundant material it receives. The debris is recycled

The Renovators Resource Inc. Typical materials seen at the Renovators Resource include windows, doors, bathtubs, hardware, lighting, plumbing, and flooring products. The company also disassembles entire wooden structures, salvaging all the reusable components and either marketing the structure whole, to be reassembled, or selling the inventory through their retail warehouse operation.

HCCDRL RECYCLING FEES

HCCDRL charges between $5 and $100 (CAD) per tonne for dropping off materials, depending on the amount of time required to sort the debris and the existing markets for feedstock material. The local landfill has established bans on certain construction materials because recycling facilities now exist to process them. Landfill tipping fees increased from $78 per tonne CAD in 1994 to $106 per tonne in 1999.

MATERIAL	TIPPING FEE $CAD PER TONNE
Concrete, brick, road asphalt, concrete block, masonry brick (painted or clean), ceramic tiles	5
Reinforced concrete	25–50
Wood (brush, clean wood, painted wood, plywood, yard waste)	50
Treated wood (pressure treated wood, creosote timbers)	75
Clean asphalt shingles	30
Clean asphalt and gravel roofing, modified bitumen roofing	35
Mixed roofing (asphalt, gravel, and insulation; asphalt shingles with wood and plastic)	75
Drywall	50
Paper products (dry cardboard, paper, waxed/soiled cardboard)	50
Metal (electrical fixtures, aluminum or steel window frames, aluminum cable, aluminum cans, brass, BX cable, steel cable, lead/zinc flashing, extruded aluminum, copper flashing/wire/pipes, telephone cable, cast-iron pipes/sinks and tubs, heavy/light steel, sheet metal, ducting)	50
Glass (mirror and window glass, glass bottles)	50
Mixed loads (any combination of the above materials, e.g., drywall with metal, wood with metal, asphalt shingles on wood, insulated vent ducts)	75–100
Other (fiberglass, Styrofoam, cellulose, KB board, or fiberboard insulation, plastic film, vinyl tiles, vinyl siding, carpet and underlay, rigid plastics, plastic light fixtures)	100

Halifax County Construction and Debris Recycling Limited (HCCDRL).

to become feedstock for products ranging from wood for hog fuel to generate power, hot and cold recycled asphalt paving, manufactured concrete products, and engineered soil matrices.

The volume of material recycled at HCCDRL may not rival that of its competitors in the United States, because C&D waste in Canada is comprised mainly of wood, drywall, asphalt shingles, and various kinds of insulation, while the emphasis in the United States is on aggregate recycling. Recycled aggregate has a well-established market, and due to its weight, the volumes processed at one company annually might be ten times that of HCCDRL. HCCDRL also carries out research and development on various recycled products, working mainly with the local department of environment and other government agencies. HCCDRL has been a pioneer in generating information to assist government agencies in establishing guidelines on the safe handling of waste C&D materials.

Clay pipe and
"speed" tile.

**Stacked adobe bricks
ready for transport.**
Earth blocks are more
commonly known in the
American Southwest as
adobe blocks. Adobes are
still produced from the
same types of materials as
they were hundreds of
years ago.

BRICK

BRICK IS ONE OF THE OLDEST—and simplest—of all building materials. It is solid, durable, and requires very little maintenance. Dating from as far back as 12,000 B.C., clay brick has quite an intriguing and exotic history. The Egyptians combined mud from the River Nile with straw 4,500 years ago to build the Sakkara pyramids, which still stand today. Baked or fired bricks have been used as a building material for more than 9,000 years. They were manufactured wherever suitable components of the mix (normally clay, sand, water, and sometimes straw), and fuel were available. Where fuel was scarce, the bricks were sun dried.

The Romans, seeing the versatility of brick, copied the idea of using bricks for construction from the Egyptians. After conquering Britain in the year A.D. 45, the Romans began using bricks, not only for housing, but for other structures, including viaducts, vaulted ceilings, and colonnades. Following the 1666 fire that ravaged the great city of London, King Charles II ordered all future buildings to be constructed of brick or stone, recognizing brick as an equal material to the popular stone, which lay in vast quantities throughout England. Although brick was not used for housing as frequently as stone in the New World, Dutch brickmakers built kilns in New Amsterdam (New York City) as early as 1628, manufacturing bricks of several shapes and colors. Canadians, having an abundance of wood and stone, did not pick up the trend of building houses of fired brick until the late 1700s.

The advantages of brick as a building material are many. Most appraisal guides give brick homes a resale value greater than those built of wood or concrete. Many brick buildings from centuries ago are still standing, and appear ageless, yet elegant. Compared to wood, brick will not rot, dent, fade, scratch, peel, or warp. The

FACTS

The world record for laying bricks was set in 1996 by a North Carolina bricklayer who laid 1,494 bricks in 60 minutes. (The wall laid by this bricklayer would equal an area 28 feet long and 10 feet high).
—*Guinness Book of World Records, 1998 edition*

VALUE OF BRICK BUILDING MATERIALS

A tremendous amount of fossil fuel energy is expended in firing clay brick. The amount of embodied energy required to produce one common brick is equivalent to that needed to produce approximately 1.2 feet of 10-inch steel beam from 100 percent recycled steel. Used brick is inexpensive, so it makes sense to reuse this valuable material wherever it is available locally and appropriate for the intended application.

BUILDING MATERIAL	PAID SALVAGE VALUE	PAID (OR CHARGED) TO RECYCLE MATERIAL +/-	NEW MATERIAL PURCHASE PRICE	USED MATERIAL PURCHASE PRICE	DENSITY OF MATERIAL	EMBODIED ENERGY TO CREATE MATERIAL
BRICK	$CAD/each[1]	$CAD/lb.[2]	$CAD/each[3]	$CAD/each[1]	lbs./cu. ft.[4]	BTU/lb.
Brick, common red	0.10	0.00	0.62–0.90	0.25–0.50	120	14,283[5]
Brick, handmade clay	0.20	0.00	n/a	0.80–1.00	150	n/a

1 Based on prices from Renovators Resource, Halifax, Nova Scotia, November 1999.

2 Based on prices from Halifax Construction & Debris Recycling Ltd., Halifax, Nova Scotia, November 1999.

3 Based on prices from Shaw Brick Store, Dartmouth, Nova Scotia, November 1999.

4 Based on values from Thomas J. Glover, *Pocket Reference,* 2nd Edition (Littleton, Colo.: Sequoia Publishing, 1995).

5 Donald Watson, *Energy Conservation through Building Design* (New York: McGraw-Hill, 1979).

fireproofing qualities of brick exceed most other building materials. Bricks can stand up to adverse weather conditions, from extreme heat to bitter cold, and in fact, absorb and store heat as a mass inside a home, as in a masonry hearth. Brick also absorbs sound better than most other comparable building products. Although not as strong in tension as in compression, and thus vulnerable to failure in seismically active areas, brickwork can be used in a variety of situations, including patios, garden terraces, fireplaces, exterior walls, and chimneys. The many styles and colors

Salvaged and cleaned stock brick, ready for reuse.

Contemporary veneer brickwork.

Practical Pig was building his house too, but he was a smart little pig that didn't mind hard work. So, he was building his house with bricks. Practical Pig wanted a stout, strong house, for he knew that the Big Bad Wolf lived in the woods nearby and little pigs were the wolf's favorite meal. So, Practical Pig kept busy, smoothing mortar and laying bricks. . . .

"I build my house of stone, I build my house of bricks,
I have no chance to sing and dance 'cause work and play don't mix."

—THREE LITTLE PIGS
(1990 DISNEY VERSION)

available offer the opportunity to create thousands of unique brickwork patterns inside and out. Finally, bricks are produced from raw materials that are abundant, inexpensive, and relatively benign ecologically to extract and discard, though relatively high in energy consumption to produce. One wonders why they have been supplanted by building products—such as cinderblocks—that are so much more expensive and toxic in production.

The Resourceful Renovator

THE MAKING OF BRICKS AND CLAY PRODUCTS

Bricks traditionally have been manufactured close to where they would be used, partly because of their bulk and weight and partly because their clay and sand constituents are found almost everywhere. As a result of an abundance of claylike soil, brickmaking is widely distributed throughout North America and world wide.

A distinction has long been made between common and stock bricks, the latter being harder, more regular, and more uniform. Stock bricks are selected from the high-temperature zones of the kiln, where they are hard-burned, of high strength, and very durable. Common bricks are from the low-temperature zones, and are usually under-burned, and of low strength and durability. Some manufacturers made stock and common bricks in different kilns or during different firings. Stock bricks were usually placed in the outer face of a load-bearing wall, because they were better able to resist weathering and gave an attractive appearance, and thus came to be called facing or face brick toward the end of the nineteenth century in the United States. Common or salmon bricks (named for their unusual pinkish orange color) were used for the inner core, or unseen part of the wall. The common bricks are

Clay products plant, c. 1930. When brickmaking developed into an industry, most cities had at least one brick plant. Bricks made locally could be sold at a lower price than those brought in from more distant factories. This has changed in the twentieth century, as differential freight rates allow bricks to be shipped from longer distances, making them competitive with locally made products.

usually more porous, slightly larger, and lighter in color than the stock brick.

Handmade bricks are generally rough and uneven in texture. Most masons prefer to build with a uniformly dimensioned brick, though early masons had to work with what was available to them. The joints of handmade brick walls were traditionally struck by a carving tool, to create an indented line about an inch deep to give a regular appearance.

Because bricks are small and relatively light, they must overlap or bond with each other to make a strong wall. Typical load-bearing brick walls are 9, 13, or more inches in thickness—multiples of the width of one brick, plus one or more joints. Bricks must also be held together by mortar having sufficient cohesive and adhesive strength. Mortar was traditionally composed of sand, water, and lime (made from burnt, crushed oyster shells, as limestone was nonexistent or very expensive to import to many areas). Modern mortar contains sand and cement.

Excavator claw marks in a clay patch. Clay is a material of varying composition formed by the erosion of rocks on the outer crust of the earth. Types of clay may differ greatly in composition and quality. Most clays are mined from open pits, though some fireclays are mined underground. After the raw material is extracted from a pit, the clay is transported to the brick factory, if not already at the same location, and is crushed to reduce it to boulder-sized pieces. The clay chunks are blended with sand or other elements to produce the required chemical and physical properties. The clay mixture is then recrushed to remove stones and to reduce the material to pieces no larger than 2 inches in diameter. Conveying equipment then transports the mixture to grinders, where it is reduced to a very fine granule and thoroughly mixed. After passing through many screens to remove uncrushed material, the clay mixture is combined with water in a pug-mill mixer.

THE MAKING OF BRICKS AND CLAY PRODUCTS

Clay products plant workers, c. 1930. After mixing, the clay is pushed through a die, which makes a continuous column of clay of the required size and shape, with the desired surface finish. The extruded column of clay is then passed through a series of automatic wirecutters, which cut the clay into bricks. The wirecutter method of manufacturing bricks is the most prevalent and is very effective at producing bricks that are uniform in size, with consistent surfaces. A diverse range of effects can be created on wirecut bricks, from slicker smooth finishes, to tumbled, sandy, and pitted surfaces. Wirecut bricks are used in a full range of applications, from small residential projects to the largest industrial sites.

After an inspection, the brick is moved into drying cars where most of the moisture is removed. The drying process causes shrinkage, which is calculated prior to the die-cutting process. Drying times can vary from 24 to 48 hours, depending on the type of clay. If bricks are to be glazed, it is often done after the drying process. Glazing consists of spraying a mixture of mineral ingredients onto one or more surfaces of the brick. The glaze will melt and fuse to the surface of the brick during the firing process, giving a glasslike surface in a variety of colors.

Brick stacked ready to be fired. Firing, or burning, the brick is a critical part of the brickmaking process. It can take up to 150 hours in a kiln to properly fire the brick. In a tunnel kiln, a trolley car stacked with bricks moves through a variety of temperature settings. The bricks are stacked on the kiln car in a certain layout, to allow circulation of the kiln gases. It can take an additional 72 hours to cool the brick, depending on the type of kiln. After the drying period, bricks are unloaded from the kiln car, sorted, graded, packaged, and then transported to brick yards, or directly to construction sites.

Machine-made brick types. A variety of styles of bricks are used in construction. The surfaces can vary from a smooth or coated face to an antique finish that has been tumbled to make the bricks look older.

Workers tilt adobe blocks on their side to dry uniformly. Mechanization has made the process more efficient. Mixers and formers can lay a field of adobe blocks out to dry in the sun in a fraction of the time required to mix the earth by hand and form the blocks one-by-one in a single wooden mold. These workers are standing the freshly laid adobe blocks on their edge so that the Sun's heat can dry all surfaces uniformly.

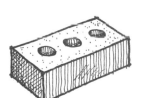

Standard hollow

Standard solid

Roman

Saxon

Giant

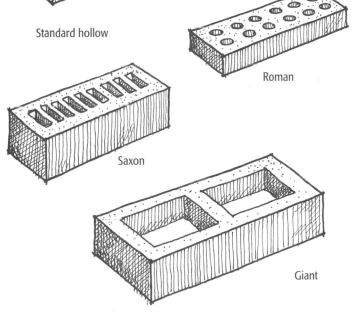

Handmade brick styles. Another, more costly method of making bricks is the soft-mud process. This is similar to the age-old process of making brick by hand-slinging the mud into individual molds for pressing. This technique has been used for generations. This process gives a unique character to each brick. Because these bricks are handmade, they are more expensive and are considered a premium product.

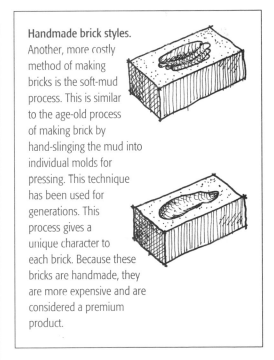

USE

This is an example of a fireplace that was used for both cooking and heating. The large opening contained the fire, where a forged iron crane supported a cast-iron pot or cauldron. The bread oven, to the upper right, was a perfect place to bake, since the entire masonry mass was well heated by the fire. Extra wood was stored below the beehive oven.

Clay brick has been used for almost as many aspects of building construction as wood, from foundations to half-round roof tiles, from fireplaces and chimneys to drainage pipes, from load-bearing walls and columns to veneer cladding and terra-cotta decorative elements, from floors and walks to archways and domes. The typical frame house of the 1800s was often built on a brick foundation wall, though many of its predecessors had wooden sills laid directly on the soil. Often these "mud"-silled buildings were later jacked up and reinforced with brick foundations. Houses built with cellars usually had their brick walls laid in a double course. An occasional cellar floor was built of brick, though often they were simply left as dirt. Brick steps down to cellars and basements were built with wood nosings, which could withstand a lot of traffic and weight. Advances in construction and the appearance of the structural steel frame changed the use of brick in construction. Thick, load-bearing masonry walls were no longer needed to support multiple stories. Ultimately, the demand for common brick dwindled and that of stock brick increased.

Brick is still an affordable material—it is normally the mason's labor rates that make it, in some cases, more costly to homeowners. Brick may still be the best choice for your new home or renovation for many reasons. It supports local industry and doesn't cause any disposal problems at the end of its lifetime—which if designed well, can last for hundreds of years.

Masonry bread oven.
Brick bread ovens are not a thing of the past; Daniel Wing and Alan Scott's book *The Bread Builders: Hearth Loaves and Masonry Ovens* describes how to build one—and how to use it to bake perfect bread. Richard Freeman built this double-walled brick bread oven in his backyard in Alabama.

New masonry heater built by Kim Aboe. Another common use for brick is in chimneys and masonry stoves. Two other options for chimney materials are steel and clay, though brick is still the most widely used.

Still used throughout North America, brick fireplaces, hearths, and chimneys are solid, thermal masses able to store heat to be distributed to a building's core.

Brick cladding used in high-rise building. Currently, brick has two distinct uses. Brick is often employed as an exterior finish, a veneer or cladding, in nonstructural wall construction in many buildings.

Popular brick bond patterns. The overlapping arrangements of bricks serve both a structural and a decorative function. Stretchers, bricks laid lengthwise, provide longitudinal bonding strength, while headers, laid across the width of the wall, bond the bricks transversely. Running bond, which consists of all stretchers, is usually used in cavity wall construction and veneered or faced walls, where transverse bonding is provided by metal ties. Common bond has a course of full-length headers at regular intervals. English bond consists of alternate courses of stretchers and headers, with the headers centered over the stretchers in the intervening courses; in veneer walls where headers do not provide structural bonding, half bricks called clipped headers may be used. In Flemish bond, each course of bricks alternates stretchers and headers, with the headers centered over the stretchers. Clipped headers may also be used. Variations on these traditional bonds may also be seen, as well as decorative patterns created by varying brick colors or mortar joint treatments, and by projecting or recessing bricks in the wall.

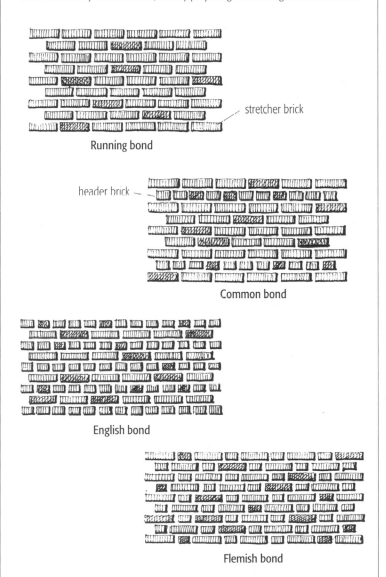

stretcher brick

Running bond

header brick

Common bond

English bond

Flemish bond

BRICK REUSE

Bricks are more commonly found at a demolition contractor's yard or on a demolition site than at a used building material store. Other masonry products, such as paving bricks, patterned bricks, or bricks with unique coloring, occasionally may be found in architectural salvage yards.

Masonry materials vary greatly in composition and appearance. Marble, brick, and some plasters are masonry materials that share certain characteristics that salvagers consider when dismantling buildings for reuse. These materials are heavy and require adequate support when preparing them for transport. All three materials are usually bonded to themselves or another surface with a mortar. Carefully removing the masonry is key, as it is somewhat fragile and may crack or break if struck sharply or dropped.

Brick can be expensive to clean, though this depends on the amount and type of mortar adhering to the bricks. Modern cement-based mortars are a lot harder than those used a century ago, and are actually stronger than old "soft" brick. If you remove old brick from a wall that has had the mortar rejointed, the bricks may break before the mortar when you try to separate them. Lime mortar should be used with older brick, but this is not a common practice, except perhaps in good-quality historical restoration work. Bricks can also be costly to transport, as the need to handle each brick makes them time consuming to load and unload, and the sheer weight may make longer distances unaffordable.

Using old bricks in exterior applications can be a complicated issue. Many people assume that since a brick wall is nearly a century old, the bricks are sound and strong and will last another hundred years. This may be true, if the bricks were laid nearly a century ago, and lime mortar was used to bond the courses. While the old, soft, red bricks have a warm color and texture, they should not be used on outdoor projects, except in a nonload-bearing wall that is well protected from the rain. Early load-bearing brick buildings used a harder brick, a stock

Salvaged bricks. Masonry products come in all shapes and sizes. Shown here, left to right from top: a cylindrical chimney crock, a rectangular chimney flue liner, an interlocking paver, two octagonal flue liners, a custom curved solid brick or lintel cap, a speed tile (a hollow wall-construction block), a saxon or five-hole brick, and two stock bricks.

Pile of cleaned, salvaged bricks. This pile of mixed brick was salvaged from a demolished school in Truro, Nova Scotia. Some of the brickwork from the 1908 building had been repaired, and cement mortar held those sections of wall together, making it more difficult to separate the bricks. However, they could be separated; it just took more time to retrieve enough bricks for a reuse project. Used brick can be acquired for anywhere from free to $0.50 CAD a brick. The company that retrieved this brick gives a discount for purchasing large volumes.

Cleaning salvaged brick. The tools required to dismantle brick are quite simple. A chisel, hammer, larger sledgehammer, and a stiff wire brush will help to loosen, break apart, and clean the mortar from the bricks.

brick, on the outer surface, and a common or salmon brick in the core of the wall. To the inexperienced eye, it will be difficult to sort the two types on a demolition site once the wall has been knocked down. Common bricks are typically larger and more porous—and ultimately susceptible to water penetration. Old brick may not have the same load-bearing capacity as new brick. The exposure to weathering and the method in which it was fired may result in a weaker brick. If you are considering using reclaimed brick in a structural capacity, hire a knowledgeable brick mason or structural engineer to inspect them prior to construction. Bricks from different sources also may be of different sizes, resulting in a rough finished appearance, though some may prefer that look.

That is not to say that you should not reuse old bricks in nonload-bearing, interior applications, or where an experienced mason can identify one type of brick from another. Used brick can add a spectacular effect to many home renovations. The color, quality, and texture of brick can enrich many spaces while retaining functionality.

SAFETY ALERT

Make sure to wear safety glasses and work gloves while cleaning salvaged brick. Edges are sharp and shards can fly up. (I have found this job to be one of the most mind-numbing tasks, along with nailpulling!)

The Resourceful Renovator

BUILD IT
WITH BRICKS

BRICK AND PLANK BOOKCASE

You very likely were a resourceful renovator in college, without even knowing it. Everyone will recognize this simplest reuse of salvaged bricks and boards as the most economical way to build an attractive bookcase. This is the bookcase design I built while at university. I visited a demolition site for a few days in a row carrying four bricks home each day in my knapsack. I found the planks in a dumpster at a nearby construction site.

You will need approximately 16 feet of 1-by-8 salvaged planking for the shelves. Do not make the bookcase more than four shelves high without additional crossbracing. Small pieces of corrugated cardboard between the bricks make a better surface for the next brick or plank. You can vary the design of the bookcase, depending on your creativity and the size of items to be stored.

Brick and plank bookcase.

Brick walkway. With the wide variety of bricks available to choose from, you must identify the type of brick you plan to reuse. One of the most common mistakes in reusing brick is to reincorporate it into landscaping without considering whether all the surfaces will be impermeable. Some bricks cannot tolerate the very severe freeze-thaw cycles in the northeastern regions of the continent. Porous brick will absorb water; which will freeze, expand, and break the brick apart. This freeze-thaw cycle can destroy bricks in only one winter, particularly if soft bricks are used for landscape work, such as walkways. About 5 percent of the carefully chosen bricks salvaged from a hospital demolition for this path have crumbled in the winters near the Atlantic Coast. A brick pathway is also difficult to shovel when covered with snow.

Durable floor made with reclaimed bricks. You can incorporate bricks even in the floors of your home. It may remind you of walking on many European streets. Brick is a suitable flooring material wherever dirt and water may be tracked into the space, such as entryways or mudrooms.

State Street brick path. Still, in a temperate climate, or with the right materials, brick can make an elegant walkway or patio. This path has withstood three upstate New York winters. Harold Mills salvaged the bricks to build it when the city of Ithaca finally paved over State Street, where the bricks had endured more than a century of horses' hooves and fifty years of motorized traffic. Refer to the Blue Stone Path project sidebar in the Stone chapter for instructions on constructing a brick walkway or outdoor patio.

OUT OF THE FRYING PAN

Reclaimed brick woodstove base. With the caveats about landscaping with bricks in a northern clime, you will still find lots of opportunities to use reclaimed bricks—anywhere they will remain dry. Brick is especially well suited to its traditional use in stoves and chimneys: Not only does it withstand high temperatures, but brick also acts as a thermal mass to store heat and release it slowly back to the surrounding room (or into the loaf of bread in a traditional masonry oven). Norbert Senf is an Ontario mason whose specialty is designing and constructing masonry heaters. These wood-burning stoves are very energy efficient, and can be made from any type of finished stone or brick. Norbert built this stove from reclaimed brick from a local demolition site.

Open-hearth fireplace built with salvaged brick. This attractive open-hearth fireplace was built from old brick recovered from a neighbor's discarded chimney. Marks and stains on the brick often can add age and warmth to brick, which can sometimes look "too new."

OUTDOOR FIREPLACE OR BARBECUE

A traditional outdoor oven or fireplace may not be the most efficient use of our wood as a fuel resource, but a summer gathering around an open fire, where the meal can be prepared, is a special occasion! Before building your outdoor fireplace, check with local officials to ensure that open fires are allowed in your municipality.

A good foundation is required for any masonry construction, to ensure that no settling or cracking will happen. The fireplace should be of double-wall construction, meaning a two-brick wide wall. This wall will create a masonry mass that holds the heat from the fire well into the evening. Old oven racks make perfect grills for the fireplace and can be found in abundance at used appliance shops.

If your bricklaying skills are better than mine, you will likely feel comfortable with a trowel, level, and mortar in your hands. If not, this may be a project where hiring a mason will save some frustration. Or, if you're adventurous, look in the library for some good, basic books on masonry techniques and construction. The tools and equipment you will require are a trowel, jointing tool, sponge, level, plumb bob and chalk line, wood mallet, brick set, and hammer. You will also need a wheelbarrow, shovel, and cement mixer to mix and transport the mortar.

Ted Mortimer salvaged the bricks for this barbeque from the remodeling site of his father's front porch. It features a convenient flat slate serving area from a local brick and stone supplier. The ½-brick-sized hole at the bottom right is a drain for rainwater.

Salvaged brick fireback. This fireback built of salvaged brick protects the kitchen wall from the woodstove's heat, and also serves as an attractive and handy storage place for pans.

BRICK RECYCLING

Pile of brick chips for landscaping. Before using brick waste as clean fill, consider better uses for the material. Brick chips can be used as a substitute for rock aggregate in asphalt paving and low-strength concrete. Small brick chips can be made by crushing old brick or defective newly manufactured brick. Brick chips can also make a very attractive landscaping material. Landscapers use brick chips along the borders of gardens, walkways, and patios. Brick chips should not to be used on paths where people will be walking barefoot because of its sharp edges.

Balancing how much it costs to replace a material, such as brick, with new stock, and how expensive it is to landfill the old material, will determine the economics of recycling. Bricks are manufactured from clay, sand, and water, all considered inert materials. Bricks without mortar attached are considered a "clean fill," and can be used to backfill excavated sites. Basically, bricks can replace the material that was taken out of the ground to manufacture them in the first place.

We should be concerned about using brick waste as a "clean fill" when a large amount of mortar is attached to the bricks. The cement component of mortar degrades to form chlorides, affecting the quality of water runoff in landfills and clean fill sites. Yet used brick and mortar are normally considered "clean fill."

THE MINNEAPOLIS
REUSE CENTER

Joyce Wisdom and the Minneapolis ReUse Center. The ReUse Center is a one-stop shopping center providing not only the materials to build with but also information for shoppers about how to use them. Homeowners aren't the only ones who venture into the ReUse Center. Customers include students working on art projects, experienced renovators, landlords, and theater set designers.

Joyce Wisdom is a woman with unlimited energy. She has been one of several driving forces behind a successful reuse, recycling, and employment initiative at the ReUse Center in Minneapolis, Minnesota. As program director, Joyce oversees one of the most successful nonprofit used building material stores in the United States.

The ReUse Center was established in October 1995 by the nonprofit organization Green Institute, a community-based economic development organization conceived in response to the demolition of twenty-eight homes and five businesses to clear a ten-acre site for the construction of a waste transfer station in 1993. The station was to be built in the Phillips neighborhood, where a very diverse group of people (Native Americans, African Americans, Cambodians, Vietnamese, Hispanic Americans, and others), were opposing the construction project. The opposition to building the transfer station prevailed when citizens cited the many negative

effects that the transfer station would pose, such as toxic fumes and other air pollution to nearby residents. Since then, the Green Institute has focussed on other issues—such as a low-employment rate, lack of affordable transportation, and many residents living at or below the poverty line—that face the Phillips neighborhood.

Upon opening the ReUse Center, Wisdom and others set five goals:

1. to create living-wage jobs in and around the Phillips neighborhood;

2. to reduce the waste stream and demand for virgin materials through the recapturing and sale of reusable building materials;

3. to make home improvements more affordable by offering a lower-cost alternative to new building materials;

4. to provide environmental education and home improvement instruction to help people become more self-sufficient; and

5. to preserve some of the architectural heritage in buildings scheduled for demolition.

To accomplish these goals, the ReUse Center gathers reusable building materials and sells them from a 26,000-square-foot retail store, at a fraction of the price of new materials. The revenues from the sales support the job creation work that the center also coordinates.

The ReUse Center also provides a resource library including a variety of do-it-yourself magazines to explain how to complete certain projects. Shoppers are invited to take part in workshops to learn about everything from hanging doors and windows, "do's and don'ts" of hiring contractors, and kitchen remodeling, to lead paint, water damage and plaster repair, and environmental issues. The classes have been successful in assisting homeowners to become more self-sufficient, while at the same time increasing people's awareness of the availability of used building materials. Somewhere in her busy schedule, Joyce oversees the publication of a

Ceramic plumbing fixtures and parts. The ReUse Center offers a limited pick-up service for customer-donated materials. This allows businesses and home-owners to donate larger quantities and high-quality materials with little effort.

ReUse Center (Green Institute)

2216 East Last Street
Minneapolis, Minnesota 55407
Phone: (612) 724-2608
Fax: (612) 724-2299
Web site: www.greeninstitute.org

Sustainability—doing more than one thing right. The ReUse Center also operates a DeConstruction Service to increase the quality and quantity of material available. Joyce has found that this service has created additional job opportunities for the neighborhood residents. "We've just recently added our third full DeConstruction crew, and anticipate that they will be very busy this year." DeConstruction crews salvage materials by dismantling residential and commercial buildings, removing a few valuable items, or taking down the complete structure.

quarterly newsletter. The ReUse Center mails 2,000 issues of *Repeat,* which is full of tips and techniques and updates from the store.

During its first year of operation, the ReUse Center earned $208,000. The second year, revenue increased by 17 percent to $244,000. In 1998, after three years in operation, the annual sales totaled $441,000—an 80 percent increase. The dramatic growth of the center was due to the implementation of the DeConstruction Service and expansion of the pick-up service. The store employs the equivalent of thirteen full-time employees and has recently become self-sufficient, earning revenues to cover direct store expenses. By the fifth year in operation, Joyce would like to see one Phillip resident graduate to a key management position in the store. She also envisions recruiting 30 to 40 percent of the new store employees from the Phillips neighborhood and selling 273,000 items, thus preventing them from being landfilled.

The used building materials industry is growing. A survey by the Used Building Materials Association and Environment Canada has shown that of the 110 facilities surveyed in 1997, only 15 existed prior to 1967. In fact, the number of facilities has doubled within the past five years. The survey also indicates that the market for used materials is still growing rapidly: one-quarter of the companies surveyed were expecting to expand their current location, or to open a second store, within the same year. Joyce Wisdom confirms this trend as she sees the ReUse Center becoming not only a store helping the people of Phillips neighborhood, but the biggest used material retailer in Minnesota.

Joyce enjoys some reclaimed stained-glass window panels. Among the more successful areas in the store are the cabinets and the doors and windows sections. As well, finishings, such as paint, wallpaper, and tile, hardware, and lawn and garden materials can be found at great prices. Many people buy insulation to help make their homes more energy efficient, while others purchase millwork to finish their renovations.

Helmut Jahn skyscraper,
Johannesburg,
South Africa.

Sand is one of the primary elements of glass. Today's glass is comprised of approximately 70 percent silica sand, 13 percent limestone, 12 percent soda ash (sodium carbonate)—all relatively low-cost raw materials—and small amounts of any of fifty other chemical compounds. Some additional substances may be used to vary the color, viscosity, and durability of glass.

GLASS

Glass is not easy to describe. The American Society for Testing and Materials (ASTM) defines glass as "an inorganic product of fusion which has cooled to a condition without crystallizing." Van Nostrand's *Scientific Encyclopedia* defines glass as "a liquid whose rigidity is great enough to enable it to be put to certain useful purposes." This "rigid liquid" definition captures the essence of the material: clear, yet hard.

Glass is a material that is truly like no other. Glass can be transparent, translucent, or opaque. It is nonporous, nonabsorptive, abrasion resistant, and impervious to the common elements and to many chemicals and liquids. It is one of the best electrical insulation materials, yet can be treated to conduct electricity and is used extensively in fiber optics. Glass's stable structure does not expand or contract in most habitable climates. Glass technically is considered a ceramic, but it stands in a class by itself.

Assortment of glass.

THE LONG HISTORY OF GLASS

The earliest glasslike material humans encountered was obsidian, a natural glass formed by volcanic activity. Early civilization fashioned this magical rock into knives, arrowheads, and ornaments. In A.D. 77, the Roman historian Pliny the Elder wrote in his encyclopedia *Naturalis Historia* that man had first produced glass by accident around 5000 B.C., when Phoenician sailors, feasting on a beach in Asia Minor, could find no stones to rest their pots upon, so they set them on blocks of soda carried in their ship as cargo. The heat of the fire turned the sand and soda into molten glass. Whether this time and date reference is accurate, the recipe is correct; glass is derived from heat, silica sand, and soda ash (sodium carbonate).

Some of the first useful glass objects date from 1500 B.C. in Egypt, where the Egyptians attached metal rods to a silica paste core, and repeatedly dipped the rods into molten glass, until glass bottles formed. The cores were later removed. Glassblowing, a Babylonian discovery, was an advance on the rod-dipping technique. Once hollow rods were tried, it was discovered that hollow shapes could be formed by blowing air into the mass. Around 250 B.C., glass vessels became easy and affordable to produce. Glass bowls and bottles replaced vessels that had previously been made of precious metals. Each piece of blown glass is unique and the small

FACT

The largest piece of installed glass in the world exists in the Saint-Gobain Company, a glass manufacturer near Compiegne, France. The piece measures 71 feet long and 9 foot 6 inches wide and was installed in 1966. (It should be noted that glass could be produced in longer pieces than this world record, though transporting the fragile glass is difficult and limits its size. For instance, a tractor-trailer can normally transport a 50-foot flatbed trailer of construction materials).

—*Guinness Book of World Records, 1998 edition*

VALUE OF GLASS BUILDING MATERIALS

The main ingredients in glass are abundant and inexpensive. However, transforming common sand into glass is an elaborate process. The raw materials must be raised to very high temperatures, and the furnaces used to manufacture glass have short life spans. While the embodied energy cost is less than many other building materials, glass is a valuable product with excellent reuse potential.

BUILDING MATERIAL	PAID SALVAGE VALUE	PAID (OR CHARGED) TO RECYCLE MATERIAL +/-	NEW MATERIAL PURCHASE PRICE	USED MATERIAL PURCHASE PRICE	DENSITY OF MATERIAL	EMBODIED ENERGY TO CREATE MATERIAL
GLASS	$CAD[1]	$CAD/lb. [2]	$CAD[3]	$CAD [1]	lbs./cu. ft.[4]	BTU/lb.
one 24 x 24 x ⅛-inch thick window glass	3.00	(0.02)	27.60	12.00	161.0	3,605[6]
one 8 x 8 inch glass block	1.50	(0.02)	12.50	4.00	161.0	3,605[6]
one 24 x 24 inch thermopane	10.00	(0.02)	65.00	30.00	161.0	13,437[5]

1 Based on prices from Renovators Resource, Halifax, Nova Scotia, November 1999.
2 Based on prices from Halifax Construction and Debris Ltd., Halifax, Nova Scotia, November 1999.
3 Typical building supply store price.
4 Based on values from Thomas J. Glover, *Pocket Reference,* 2nd Edition (Littleton, Colo.: Sequoia Publishing, 1995.

5 Donald Watson, *Energy Conservation through Building Design* (New York: McGraw-Hill, 1979).
6 George Baird and Michael Donn, *Energy Performance of Buildings* (Boca Raton: CRC Press, 1984).

air bubbles, along with the traces left by the rod on the bottom of the object, are signs that differentiate it from a machine-made glass object.

The history of window glass is not quite as long as the history of glassmaking, but it does date from as early as the Roman Empire (753 B.C.–A.D. 476). The first use of glass for building construction was simply to cover small wall openings, though after many unsuccessful attempts, the Romans still could not replace their shutters with window glass. Their attempts to cast transparent flat glass to enclose or ornament their homes didn't work, so they used thin, translucent sheets of alabaster to cover wall openings.

Lead and glass quarrels. After numerous trials and errors, some houses were fitted with diamond-shaped panes, known as quarries or quarrels, held in place by lead strips. Soon after, wrought iron casement frames were developed.

Gothic window salvaged from a dismantled church. The art of glassmaking advanced slowly. Gothic cathedrals of the late twelfth century featured small bits of colored glass in complex designs (quite an advanced fashion), though at this point window glass was still rare and prohibitively expensive. During the thirteenth and fourteenth centuries, Venetian glassmakers became world renowned for their products—thin, clear *cristallo*. In England, during the great deforestation of the fifteenth century, glassmakers changed their fuel source from wood to coal. When lead oxide was added later in the century, the resultant glass became a more solid, heavy, and durable product, compared to that being made in Venice.

Early wood frame window. Wood replaced metal as the frame to hold the glass. As the panes were still relatively small, a multipane frame was developed.

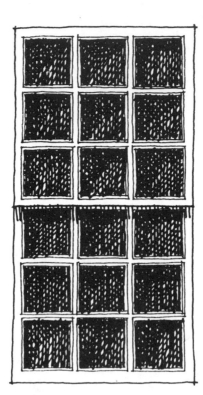

Sash window. Operable sash windows in a wooden frame replaced the early fixed iron and wood frame window. The sash, normally sliding up and down, was still configured with multiple small panes of glass. As window glass became less costly and more common in the late eighteenth century, demand increased for larger panes. Better-quality glass, with fewer blisters and striations, was being developed. Many of the successful glass houses hired European workers, whose reputation for glassmaking was world renowned.

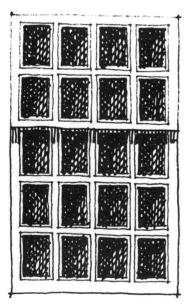

Twenty-pane and four-pane sashes. Flat glass for windows was still quite rare for most of the seventeenth and eighteenth centuries. In the 1620s, window glass made its way across the Atlantic to North America, but continued to be imported in large quantities throughout the seventeenth to nineteenth centuries. The first North American attempts at making glass were in Jamestown, Virginia, in 1608 and 1621. These trials failed, and so did the hopes to export the product back to England.

Improved air-compressing technology led to better and flatter panes of glass. In 1830, it took only four panes of glass to cover the same area that twenty-four panes covered in 1730. During this time, prices dropped and glass-enclosed "wind eyes" were becoming more common. Despite the advantage of increased production and cheaper material, acquiring glass still depended, to a large extent, upon one's economic circumstances. As late as the 1850s, many buildings still did not contain a single piece of window glass.

Bull's eye

Crown glassmaking method. The two principal techniques for manufacturing window glass in the seventeenth and eighteenth centuries were the "cylinder glass" and the "crown glass" methods. The crown method consisted of blowing a large bubble, attaching a rod to the end opposite the blowpipe, then cracking off the blowpipe,

which left a hole in the bubble. This hole was enlarged with a paddle and by reheating and twirling the piece, until a disc of flat glass, or crown, was made. Occasionally the remaining rod mark, referred to as the bull's eye, was used in transoms, where light was needed, but where a clear view through the glass was not required.

Typical cutting pattern for crown glass.

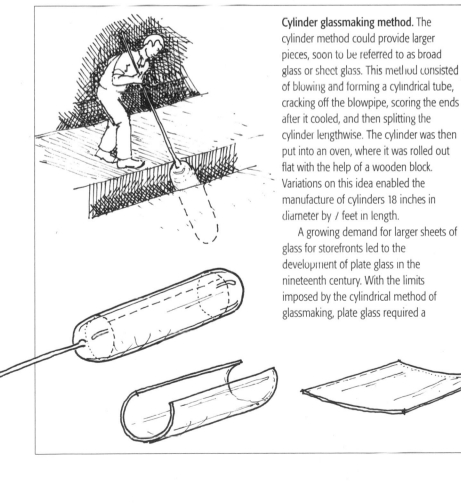

Cylinder glassmaking method. The cylinder method could provide larger pieces, soon to be referred to as broad glass or sheet glass. This method consisted of blowing and forming a cylindrical tube, cracking off the blowpipe, scoring the ends after it cooled, and then splitting the cylinder lengthwise. The cylinder was then put into an oven, where it was rolled out flat with the help of a wooden block. Variations on this idea enabled the manufacture of cylinders 18 inches in diameter by 7 feet in length.

A growing demand for larger sheets of glass for storefronts led to the development of plate glass in the nineteenth century. With the limits imposed by the cylindrical method of glassmaking, plate glass required a

different manufacturing process. The grinding and polishing equipment, initially water powered, advanced with steam power, and later electricity. This made grinding and polishing heavy glass plates much easier. This product was widely used by business and commercial building owners during this era. The first wave of plate glass used in North America was imported from France. One of the first attempts to make it in America was in 1853 at the Lenox Glass Works in Berkshire, Massachusetts. This company made rough and polished plate glass until 1872, when the company failed. North America continued to make glass into the twentieth century, though much of the glass used was still imported.

Continuous ribbon of float glass at Pittsburgh Plate Glass Company (PPG). Today, glass is manufactured by the float process, developed in 1959. Molten glass is poured onto a bath of liquid tin, which gives the glass an exceptionally brilliant finish. The material is spread out to make a wide, flat ribbon of glass that goes untouched until it hardens. A controlled stretching force is applied as the glass cools to create two parallel surfaces. The product is cooled until it is durable enough to withstand conveyance on rollers. The large ribbon enters an oven to be heated to a temperature that relieves the stress that the cooling process causes. The ribbon then continues down the conveyor to be cut, inspected, and packaged. The glass is cut from this ribbon for use in flat form, or it may be bent, laminated, tempered, or coated through other fabrication processes, to give the glass additional applications.

The advantage of this process is that it is very economical, compared to earlier techniques, because no polishing is required. In addition, the glass can be coated with transparent metal or metal oxide films to reduce glare or heat transmission. These coatings are a cost savings to the overall performance of a building, as they minimize both heat gain and loss.

Cross-section of a double-glazed window and a quadruple-glazed window . Today, the glass industry has advanced leaps and bounds beyond the initial small diamond-shaped pieces of glass used in housing. A concern for energy efficiency and heat loss in and around window and door openings has put pressure on the industry to make a product with a higher insulation value. The development of double, triple, and even quadruple pane units is improving the insulative or R-value of windows. The glass panes are being twinned with transparent metal coatings, called low-e (low emissivity) films, to reduce heat transfer. As well, argon and other inert gases are being sealed between the glass layers to improve their thermal efficiency. Early attempts to build these sealed units were not very successful because of the problem with the seal between the glass and metal frame. This would allow moist air to infiltrate the cavity, causing condensation. It is difficult and costly to repair these units, because once moisture is trapped between the panes of glass, it can actually corrode the glass and cause minor etching. The frame can be removed and the panes resealed, but this may be more expensive than buying a new, more efficient unit.

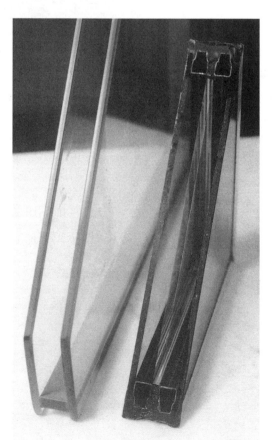

FACT

The typical float glass furnace is 165 feet long, 30 feet wide, and 4 feet deep. It can hold 1,200 to 1,500 tons of molten glass. For economic reasons, most furnaces operate 24 hours a day, 365 days a year.

Modern stained-glass window by Susan MacKenzie. Stained glass is a common, decorative type of window glass that came into fashion in the 1830s. Some stained-glass works are also painted, to add to the colorful effect of the glass. Stained glass is incorporated into construction in a number of places, usually in and around the entry system, over door panels, side lights, windows, and partitions.

STAINED GLASS

New stained-glass church window. This design was created for the re-erected century-old church featured in the Stone chapter.

STAINED-GLASS COMPOUNDS AND COLORS

COMPOUND	COLOR
Cobalt Oxide	Blue
Copper Oxide	Green
Manganese Oxide	Violet
Gold or Selenium	Red/Pink
Uranium Oxide, Cadmium Oxide, or Silver	Yellow
Ferric Oxide	Brown
Iridium Oxide	Black
Calcium Phosphate and/or Aluminum Oxide	Milky White

It is interesting to note that gold was used in stained-glass making. Next time you see an old piece of stained glass, note the amount of pink and red used compared to the other colors in the piece. Due to its expense, red stained glass was often used only as an accent color. Less-expensive substitutes are used to create these colors in modern stained glass.

USE

The way that we most commonly observe windows is by looking through them in our homes. The panes of glass are typically a few feet wide by a few feet high. Glass gives us many opportunities to greatly enhance our homes and lifestyles. Window designs vary widely, as some designers attempt to reproduce earlier proportions of small diamond panes and traditional "six-over-six" windows, while others incorporate large, uninterrupted panes of glass to enhance the view, as well as to admit light and air.

Various ways to incorporate glass into a house. A number of innovative ways to utilize glass in housing have been borrowed from commercial and industrial design and trends. For example, skylights and sun tubes, meant to allow light through the roof structure, can light the interior of a building and create the illusion of larger living spaces.

Picture windows provide a large proportion of glass to wall area, which is increased and uninterrupted, allowing for improved vistas. Sliding glass doors are a further development of picture windows, with the added ability to use them as entrances. The advanced low-e coatings and reflective tintings have helped cure the problem of heat loss through large windows.

Clerestory windows, horizontal bands of glass placed in the wall, are commonly used in churches; this allows light to enter above head level.

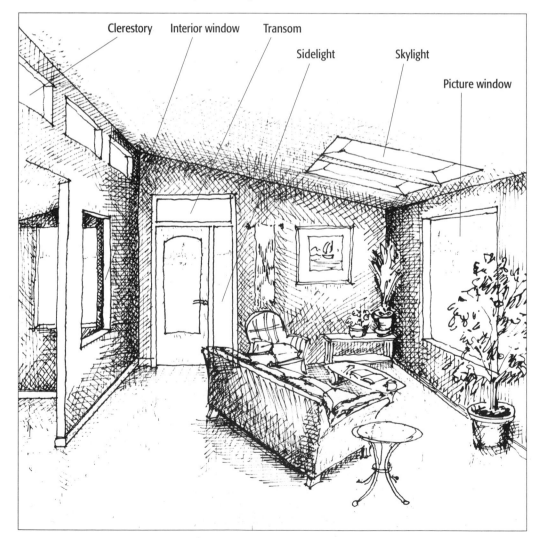

Clerestory   Interior window   Transom

Sidelight   Skylight

Picture window

The Fagus-Werk building, Alfeld-an-der-Leine, Germany.
The curtain wall system, first used by architect Walter Gropius in 1913, is a type of construction with no exterior load-bearing walls. The structural system is placed away from the exterior of the building, to allow for a complete face, or facade, of glass. This system has been developed further and is used throughout the world for high-rise design.

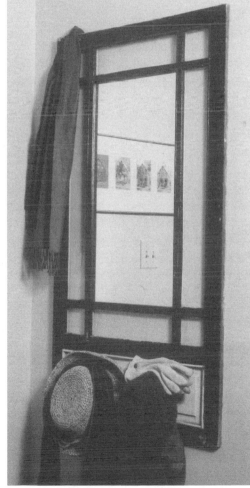

Salvaged window used as entry hall mirror.

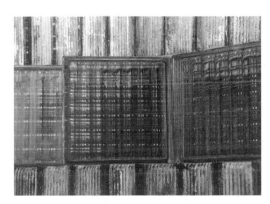

Glass blocks. Glass block is installed in a manner similar to masonry brick, but has the added feature of transmitting light. Glass block is more commonly seen in industrial buildings, though recently it is being used more frequently in residential design. The block, usually available in 4-inch, 8-inch, or 12-inch-square pieces with a 4-inch thickness, can be used in exterior walls, shower enclosures, or privacy partitions. Glass blocks are available in a number of styles, from frosted and patterned to clear blocks. All of the patterns are available with a white or green tinted glass insert to reduce brightness and heat gain if the block is located in direct sunlight.

The palace of Versailles used mirrors as an interior design method of expanding space during the reign of Louis XIV. Even earlier than that, the Egyptians were known to have used mirrors in pyramids to reflect light into the structures. This "doubling of space" happens when the eye and brain are fooled into thinking the space extends through the mirror. Mirrors are used in many architectural situations, from sliding partition walls and closet doors to backing for furniture.

GLASS
REUSE

Discontinued "new" windows at used prices. You may find two typical general categories of windows at used building material stores. The first includes new products that are discontinued stock or mismatched custom orders, which were obtained directly from the manufacturer. These windows will likely be thermopane units with a vinyl, wood, or metal frame. You may find great prices on this type of window, as long as the dimensions of your window opening can be adjusted to what is available.

Richard O. Byrne, in "Conservation of Historic Window Glass," writes,

> Often neglected, carelessly treated and broken, and replaced with inappropriate materials, historic window glass is becoming a rare architectural feature. . . . Glass is a two-way visual experience. Sunlight playing on the exterior facade of a structure with its original glass intact presents a unique and lively visual statement. One also receives a unique impression looking out through historic glass. The world is softened, distorted, and given visual movement as the viewer moves. To needlessly destroy this visual characteristic greatly diminishes the quality of the expression a structure articulates. Unlike paint and other renewable surfaces, glass is often the only "original" visual element that gives the same view to each viewer from generation to generation.

Often, however, the best use of salvaged single-pane windows is not to reincorporate them as exterior windows. Single-pane windows are not as energy efficient as the newer models. This may not be as important when using old windows in workshops or cottages, where continual heating is not a concern. Many homeowners have taken windows from their homes and reused them in their cottages, to slowly upgrade the appearance and security of the building.

Salvaged window selection at used building material store. The second category is windows salvaged from demolished or renovated buildings. These windows can vary in age, depending on the vintage of the building from which they were salvaged. You may find beveled glass, stained glass, or multipane windows perfectly suited to your renovation.

Most of this category are single-pane windows with wooden frames, though some early thermopane units are now for sale, because improvements in window technology have developed more energy-efficient units. Be aware of the condition of the wood frame. Look for windows with little or no water damage. As well, thermopane units can be cracked or have broken seals—and the repair of the glass can be as costly as the price of the used window.

Before window was added. One of the most exciting design possibilities for a renovation project is modifying the interior of an older building without affecting the integrity of the structure. Most renovations work to adapt the existing floor plan for more usable space or improved circulation. One aspect not always considered is the natural lighting of the rooms. Interior spaces are often left in the dark, far from a well-lit window. One fantastic use for old single or multipane windows is in an interior wall to enable light to reach further into the building. Interior windows are not widely used, though they can open up interior spaces visually while still having the barrier of glass between spaces. Interior windows that can open and close give the homeowner much more flexibility when it comes to using a space.

Storm window used as operable interior window. This dining room used to be a very dark. The west window (not shown) once allowed great sunsets to cast light into the room, until a new house was built next door, limiting the light entering the room. This storm window, now hinged as an operable window, lets light in through what was a pass-through from the original pantry kitchen.

Salvaged single-hung thermopane windows in renovated sunroom. The same homeowners also bought a number of different-sized thermopanes at a used building material store to incorporate into the small pantry kitchen, which they converted into a sunroom.

The Resourceful Renovator

Salvaged multipane window heat register. Windows can also become attractive heat registers. This window is used in a second-story bedroom, which is located adjacent to the stairwell. As heat naturally travels upward, this window can be opened to allow more heat into the room. Old farmhouses commonly had cast-iron grates in the floor, to allow the heat from the cookstoves or fireplaces on the main floor to rise upward—very basic heating systems still being used today!

Numerous salvaged windows in corporate office. A television production company recently used numerous salvaged single-paned windows in a renovation, including the twelve seen in the rear wall of the atrium space. The windows add variety to the inner courtyard effect, and work well to allow a partial view and light into the open space, without allowing sound and privacy to be sacrificed. This project designer first obtained the windows and then worked their dimensions into the renovation plan. This is often the best way to incorporate old windows, or any other salvaged material, as waiting to find a particular-sized item may limit the possibilities within the project.

WINDOWS
OUT OF CONTEXT

CABINET WITH WINDOW DOOR

Seeing piles of old windows being wrecked at a demolition can be a disheartening sight. Often the windows that are salvaged are those that have an interesting pattern, such as nine-pane windows, or ones with colored glass. There doesn't seem to be much interest in the plain old single-pane window. This cabinet makes great use of an old salvaged window, and promotes the fact that it is old by leaving the original paint to show through. Build the carcass of the cabinet using 1 x 8-inch planking for the sides and cover molding for the trim. Assemble the cabinet using plugged-screw connections (see page 28 for details). You may leave the back of the cabinet open, or finish it with old wainscoting or wood paneling. Use old butt hinges to attach the window, and a window lock for the latch. Tools required for this job are a circular saw, mitre box and handsaw, power drill, glue, sandpaper, and wood plugs.

PICTURE FRAMES

Any renovations to an older home with lath and plaster walls usually result in some of the lath being removed. This wood is usually very dry and makes great kindling for your fireplace. Before you burn your spare pieces, though, how about using it to build some simple picture frames? You can use old glass over a matted photograph, old map, or artwork, or set an old mirror into the frame.

Clean some lath, so that it is free of nails and plaster, and cut the pieces with a handsaw or jigsaw to create a frame like the one shown here. Use metal

mending plates, available in most hardware stores, to hold the thin pieces of lath together at the back of the frame. Trim the edges of the frame and nail them together with finishing nails. Picture wire, two threaded eye hooks, and heavy cardboard are all you need to finish and hang the frame.

ON A HORTICULTURAL NOTE

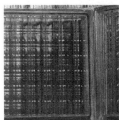

Coldframe on side of house. Single-pane windows can improve the productivity of your garden, by providing a transparent weather barrier for your plants. A coldframe can extend the growing season, by allowing you to start your plants earlier in the spring and protecting them on frosty nights in the fall. A coldframe is basically a five-sided glass box that heats up from the Sun's warmth and holds the heat longer into the evening than would normally happen in the open air. Building a coldframe can be a very affordable project that takes advantage of single-pane windows that are being tossed out at most renovation sites. Either wooden or aluminum frame windows are perfect candidates for coldframes.

ALUMINUM WINDOW COLDFRAME

When choosing windows, try to configure the windows into a box, so that all sides meet evenly. (For example, four 16 x 28-inch windows for the sides, and one 28 x 28-inch window for the top would make an easy-to-assemble coldframe.)

   If you use a larger wood sash window for your coldframe, the sides can be built of wood planking. Though not quite as effective as a five-sided glass box, wood sides can easily be built from scrap 1 x 8 or 1 x 10-inch planking.

Hinge on wooden coldframe. Other materials and tools required to build a coldframe are 1 x 2 wood strips for mounting the top lid, hinges, metal screws (for aluminum frames), wood screws, chain (to hold the lid in an open position), a handsaw, and a power drill.

Scott and Helen's greenhouse. If you are considering using salvaged windows in a larger project, such as a greenhouse from old aluminum storm windows, Scott Fotheringham and Helen Brown have some building techniques to share. These two energetic Nova Scotia farmers built their own storage building for their organic garden crops. "We carefully looked around for the most economical and durable method of building a greenhouse, to attach to our storage building. When a large quantity of same-sized aluminum-framed windows became available, they seemed like the easiest material to work with. The aluminum frame is easy to drill or nail through to attach to the wooden frame, and a panel can more easily be replaced, when compared to choosing larger panels of glass or plastic sheeting. As well, reusing windows is just an example of the larger goal of living lightly off this earth . . . and it complements our endeavor of organic gardening."

OTHER USES FOR GLASS

Salvaged 12-inch block entry. The entry also incorporates salvaged 12-inch blocks and is a bright backdrop for the café customers.

Salvaged conical light fixture. Glass lightshades also come in and out of style, as interior decorating trends change. These conical glass shades are attached by three chains to a metal base. Reusing lighting fixtures is relatively simple.

SAFETY ALERT

Be aware that any fluorescent tube fixture made before 1972 may have PCBs and mercury vapor in the unit's ballast. Most regions restrict the disposal of the PCBs, and you may get caught with a costly disposal charge.

Salvaged glass block used in counter base. Glass blocks can add interest to a renovation without great cost. The fact that glass blocks can also be used in a structural application adds to their versatility. This coffee shop owner decided to incorporate salvaged glass block in a variety of ways. The base for the main counter in the café is built with 8-inch blocks, creating an attractive curve.

RECYCLING

The two main types of glass are flat glass, used for windows, and container glass. Recycling facilities for bottle and container glass are well established, yet very few exist to accommodate window glass, because window glass melts at a different temperature than container glass. Foreign objects in the crushed waste glass, or cullet, used in the production of container glass from recycled glass, can cause weaknesses in the walls of new glass bottles.

Because glass is impermeable and compatible with drainage material such as gravel, crushed glass is perfect for use in drainage systems, base course materials, and fill. The U.S. National Standards Plumbing Code has approved the use of recycled glass cullet in storm drain construction. New Westminster, British Columbia, uses recycled glass cullet in the foundations under new or replacement sidewalks. Landscape architects are beginning to use cullet and ground glass for pathway and driveway surfaces. This cullet currently is comprised primarily of bottle glass, though current research and testing projects are using window glass as a component in this mixture.

Glass cullet is also being tested by various departments of transportation for use in road construction. The city of Norwalk, Connecticut, performed tests on a section of road paved with "Glasphalt," a fine aggregate used in bituminous asphalt paving. The surface durability passed all tests. In most regions, the price of Glasphalt is the same as conventional asphalt. The added incentive is the saving to regional recycling programs and landfill costs. It is estimated that in the state of Connecticut, landfilling glass has a net cost of $69 U.S. ($110 CAD) per ton for the taxpayer. Connecticut and New York City have been using anywhere from 10 to 50 percent cullet in their paving mix since the early 1990s.

One company in Saskatchewan, Canada, recycles bottle glass for use in road paint. The glass content makes the painted lines on the roads visible at night. Another firm in Ottawa, Ontario, called Ottawa Fibre Inc., uses a 50 percent mixture of recycled glass from post-commercial and post-industrial supplies in their insulation and ceiling tile products. The Amherst Glass Works, a new business in Nova Scotia, is turning waste window glass into decorative products.

Still, very little window glass is being recycled. The goal of improving the percentage of this material being recycled must be balanced against the priorities of other recycling projects.

Glass ready to be cleaned and ground as cullet.

Typical glass containers in a blue bag program.

BEAR RIVER'S OAKDENE CENTRE

Bear River, Nova Scotia, is a community with spirit. It is also the home of many of the province's well-known artists and the proud owner of one of Canada's latest solar-aquatic sewage treatment plants. This plant provides an environmentally sound, water-saving approach to sewage treatment, while re-creating a marsh environment with many plants and flowers. One of Bear River's most recent success stories, though, is the saving of a schoolhouse and its re-opening as Oakdene Centre.

The Oakdene School—a two-and-a-half-story, wood-frame building with eight classrooms, a gymnasium, two offices, washrooms, and lots of interior wood details and character—had not been occupied since 1993. It had been put on the market twice in a public tender, but didn't receive any reasonable offer. The school closure was yet another loss for the village of 750 people, which had seen the demise of many of its services in the early 1980s, including the drugstore, railway station, military base, and local bank. Then in 1995, Robbie Bays, spokesperson for a group of concerned Bear River residents, recommended that the vacant building be saved and become a much-needed community center. In the end, officials agreed to deed the building to a nonprofit community group—The Bear River Community Craft and Recreation Facility Society—for one dollar.

The community pulled together and took on the renovation of what is now called Oakdene Centre, with Robbie Bays as project

Oakdene Centre before. The list of required renovations was immense. Almost every surface of the building needed to be scraped, cleaned, or refinished. The entire exterior of the building was stripped of paint, shingles repaired, and then resealed. A new peak, built from salvaged timbers, was added on to the existing roof, which leaked badly. Each window had to be re-puttied, and some panes replaced.

Keeping the original windows has retained the wonderful appearance of the structure. Even the bell tower has a recycling history: the bell, from a Dominion Atlantic Railway locomotive, was given to the school when it was built in 1934.

Dismantling activity at military buildings in Cornwallis, Nova Scotia. Many of the materials required to renovate Oakdene came from donations, but the majority of the much-needed lumber was salvaged from a storage shed at a nearby closed military base. The roof and its new peak were rebuilt with reclaimed 2 x 6s and 1 inch boards.

manager. The goal was to preserve Oakdene as a center for education and recreation for the benefit of the people of Bear River. Taking on a project like this would normally require an open wallet to convert the 12,000-square-foot school into a usable, multiservice public building.

Oakdene Community Centre
Bear River, Nova Scotia, Canada
Project Manager, Robbie Bays
Phone: (902) 467-3939
E mail: oakdene@glinx.com

While most of the materials were donated, a large part of the value of this project was labor. Labor programs from the Human Resources Development office and the local Social Services Department provided the opportunity for people to gain skills in building and renovating. People who had to pay fines to the police department could fulfill their obligations with community service at the center. Coordinating the effort took an immense amount of Bays's time. "We approached every source of funding that we knew of to participate. We've had over $100,000 (CAD) of assistance from various sources for labor to date."

The center was able to rescue over one hundred various-sized thermopane window units from a glass company that had recently closed its operations, saving an estimated $6,000 in materials from the landfill. The Bear River Community Craft and Recreation Facility Society is currently working with architecture students to design a solarium on the back of the building that will incorporate the thermopanes.

The total cost of this project was nearly $250,000, which included the assistance from employment programs, and has an economic impact of well over $1,000,000. But the unquantifiable value of Oakdene Centre is the satisfaction enjoyed by many people of Bear River, who now have a place to come together to plan their next step to continuing community spirit.

Oakdene Centre after.
The Oakdene Centre now provides space for a variety of programs, including a music society, a women's business center, a weekly coffee house, a public computer center, a darkroom, boys' and girls' groups, volleyball, dancing, and badminton. Eight classrooms have also been renovated and rented to subsidize overhead costs. The spaces have become studios for many sculptors, potters, and other craftspeople.

CER

Handmade tiles with embossed, trailed glazing.

Salvaged ball- and claw-foot cast-iron bathtubs for sale.

AMICS

THE WORD *CERAMICS* COMES from "Keramos"—Greek for "pottery." This Greek word is related to the Sanskrit word meaning "to burn." Ceramics are defined as products made from inorganic materials having nonmetallic properties, usually fired at high temperatures. This technical definition encompasses a number of products, from dinnerware, vases, and artwork, to a wide variety of construction materials.

The most enduring characteristic of ceramics is durability. Ceramics are durable in three ways—chemically, mechanically, and thermally. Chemically, ceramic products are resistant to almost all acids, alkalis, and solvents. Unlike most metals, ceramics are also unaffected by oxygen (they do not rust or corrode). Mechanically, they are very strong and hard; the compressive strength of some ceramic is approximately 50,000 to 100,000 pounds per square inch. This quality makes them abrasion resistant, which is why they are desirable as a flooring material. Thermally, ceramics have the ability to withstand high temperatures, making them appropriate for linings or conductors in electrical and heating implements.

As practical, versatile, and attractive as ceramic products can be, they are also extremely expensive to manufacture—in embodied energy, that is. The ticket price of a porcelain fixture seems unreasonably low when the environmental costs have been taken into consideration. An enormous amount of fuel must be consumed to fire clay products to the intensely hot temperatures necessary to produce the desired hard-glazed surfaces. Fortunately, the same durability that makes ceramics valuable the first time around means these items last to be reused in your home, either in their original function, or for a new purpose.

Do not keep anything in your home that you do not know to be useful, or believe to be beautiful.

—WILLIAM MORRIS

CERAMICS

MAKING MUD PIES:
THE HISTORY OF CERAMIC

Ceramic dates back as far as the fourth millennium B.C., in Egypt, where tiles were first used to decorate houses. In those days, clay tiles were dried or baked by the sun-hence the name terra cotta, meaning "burnt earth." The first tiles were blue and contained copper oxide. Ceramics were also produced in Mesopotamia as early as 4000 B.C. These early ceramics were decorated in blue and white stripes, and later displayed more patterns and colors.

The European clay potters in the sixteenth and seventeenth centuries A.D. were not satisfied with the finished surfaces of their ceramics, so they looked to the Chinese, who had developed porcelain—a translucent, white, and fully vitrified ceramic—hundreds of years earlier. The Europeans discovered that Chinese porcelain was not made from a red clay, but from a white base known as kaolin. The word *kaolin* is a Chinese word meaning "high hill"—where the clay was originally mined. The first European to develop this "china clay" was Johann Friedrich Bottger, in

VALUE OF CERAMIC BUILDING MATERIALS

This chart gives an overview of the current market value for certain ceramic building materials. Similar to other materials such as glass, wood, or brick, much more value can be gained by reusing an existing product rather than recycling or replacing it with new material. One can emphasize the value of ceramics three ways. First, ceramics are usually used for interior finishings and fixtures, which tend to have higher values per unit than most framing, foundation, or insulation materials. So reusing a sink, for example, can save up to 1,000 percent of the cost of a new fixture. Second, the amount of energy consumed to manufacture ceramic products is very high, similar to that of glass and brick manufacture. The embodied energy requirements to replace that sink will add a higher environmental burden than replacing a wooden 2 x 4. Third, ceramics presently have little recycled value. Though ceramics can be used safely as clean fill, salvaged stone and rubble are much less expensive to obtain as fill products.

BUILDING MATERIAL	PAID SALVAGE VALUE	PAID OR (CHARGED) TO RECYCLE MATERIAL +/-	NEW MATERIAL PURCHASE PRICE	USED MATERIAL PURCHASE PRICE	DENSITY OF MATERIAL	EMBODIED ENERGY TO CREATE MATERIAL
CERAMIC	$CAD/each[1]	$CAD/lb.[2]	$CAD/each[3]	$CAD/each[1]	lbs./cu. ft.[4]	BTU/sq. ft.
12 x 12 ceramic tile	0.20	0.00	2.50–15.00	1.00–5.00	120.0–150.0	62,682[5]
6 x 6 ceramic tile	0.10	0.00	1.00–4.00	0.25–1.50	120.0–150.0	62,682[5]
Toilet	10.00	0.00	118.00–199.00	25.00–50.00	150.0	n/a
Wall-hung porcelain sink	5.00	0.00	49.00	20.00–25.00	150.0	n/a

1 Based on prices from Renovators Resource, Halifax, Nova Scotia, November 1999.

2 Based on prices from Halifax Construction & Debris Recycling Ltd., Halifax, Nova Scotia, November 1999.

3 Typical building supply store purchase price.

4 Based on values from Thomas J. Glover, *Pocket Reference,* 2nd Edition (Littleton, Colo.: Sequoia Publishing, 1995).

5 Donald Watson, *Energy Conservation through Building Design* (New York: McGraw-Hill, 1979).

Dresden, Germany, in 1708. Bottger established a factory for producing white porcelain at nearby Meissen, which has become an important center for porcelain production.

Ceramics were produced in North America as early as 1641 in Salem, Massachusetts, beginning with the manufacture of simple objects such as urns, crocks, pitchers, and plates. These objects were made from red, brown, and yellow burnt clays. The clays were finished with glazes made of lead oxide, flint, and clay mixtures.

The manufacture of ceramics is similar to that of bricks and other clay building products described in an earlier chapter. They all

A variety of industrially produced ceramic tiles. Throughout the centuries, the tile manufacturing and decoration process has been mechanized. In the early days, each tile was hand formed and painted; therefore each piece was different. Today, ceramic tile is generally neither handmade nor hand-painted. Manufacturing techniques have advanced so far that a human does not enter the process until the tile is installed in a building. However, manufactured tiles cannot compare to the beauty of historic or contemporary handmade tiles.

start with a clay base that produces a solid unit when fired at extreme temperatures. Over the centuries, the use of ceramics has been developed to include a variety of glazes and finishes on the clay body to suit various requirements. Porcelain, porcelain enamels, vitreous china, refractories, and white wares are all derivatives of the initial discovery of fired clay.

Manufacturing of ceramic items such as toilets follows the same process as ceramic tiles. Prior to the industrial boom after World War II, most sinks and toilets were made from clay, fired and glazed numerous times to make a solid, water-repellent surface.

Glaze trailing (filling in glaze between raised pattern areas) on bisque-fired redware. Clay is a hydrated aluminosilicate, and is the end product of weathered, feldspathic rock, with the most important mineral being kaolin. Clay is the material that gives a ceramic the plasticity that facilitates its fabrication into the desired form prior to firing in a kiln. Flint, a form of silicon dioxide that is usually produced from quartzite sand or rock, is ground into fine particles to give the clay and the final product the desired properties. Feldspar is used as a "flux" in the ceramic industry. A flux starts to melt at the lowest temperature during the firing process, therefore acting as the cement that gives the ceramic body strength. Many other naturally occurring minerals and some synthetically produced chemicals, including magnetite, iron oxide, cobalt, borax, lead, and silicon, are also used as raw materials in the ceramic industry.

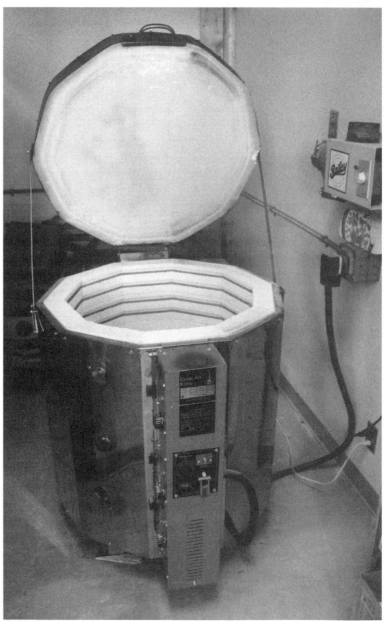

A small electric kiln. A kiln is merely an enclosure for containing heat and the material to be heated. The sources of heat are usually electrical elements, gas, oil, or coal. The enclosure itself is built of ceramic refractories (materials that resist high temperatures), while the inner lining is composed of even more resistant refractories. The ceramic floor and wall tile industry uses tunnel kilns, which are from 80 to over 300 feet long. The tiles travel on cars, belts, or sliding slabs through the firing kiln, gradually heating as they progress slowly toward the center of the kiln, and slowly cooling as they approach the tunnel exit. To maximize efficiency and economy, to keep the product uniform, and to minimize lag time, a constant flow of tiles must pass through these kilns twenty-four hours a day.

Tilemaker Sherry Schalm applies glaze to a bisqued tile. After an initial, or bisque, firing, a handmade ceramic tile can be glazed by a variety of methods prior to a second firing to fuse the glaze.

Glaze chemistry is a complex field requiring many experiments with temperature, time, and chemical mixtures.

Maiolica painted tiles. This style uses colored pigments placed on top of a white, opaque glaze.

Majolica painted tiles. This method involves tinted, but transparent glazes over a white, opaque glaze.

This technique was costly and the glaze was susceptible to fine spiderlike cracks, called crazing. Today, most plumbing fixtures are made from vitreous china, which is manufactured from ball clay, china clay, silica, and a fluxing agent. The advantage of vitreous china is that the base of the clay body and the glaze material contract and expand at the same rate and thus can be kiln-fired together. The finish of vitreous china turns to a glassy solid when fired and is waterproof, stain-proof, and will not burn, rot, rust, or promote bacterial growth.

USE

The variety of building materials made from ceramics is broader than most people realize. The list includes floor, wall, and ceiling tile, bath and shower tile, exterior cladding, and roofing tile; plumbing fixtures such as sinks, toilets, and bathtubs; door and shelving hardware and bathroom fixtures; and various electrical and electronic components, such as insulators for wiring, pipes, and casings.

Custom countertop and backsplash tile by Sherry Schalm. Ceramic tile provides an attractive surface in both residential and institutional applications. The choice of colors and sizes is almost limitless. All tile has a hard, permanent surface that is easily cleaned and maintained, which is its biggest selling point. Tile is finding a wider variety of uses other than just interior floors and walls—it is often used in exterior cladding applications, and as decorative artwork on walls, or as part of furnishings.

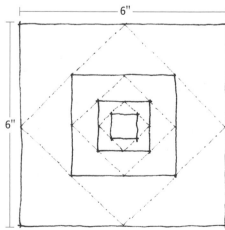

The basis of sizes for common square tiles of less than 36 square inches is shown.

THE BEAUTY AND VERSATILITY OF CERAMIC TILES

Tiles are small ceramic surfacing units that are usually flat, and can be glazed or unglazed. Tiles can be made from red or white clay bodies. The surface finish that a tile retains and the surface vitrification will indicate what level of moisture can be absorbed. Tiles can be used in a variety of applications and are normally classified in four categories: glazed wall tile, mosaic tile, quarry tile, and paver tile. Most homeowners would be familiar with glazed tile, as that is what would be found on the floors and walls of bathrooms, kitchens, and utility areas. Glazed wall tile can also be used for ceilings and fireplaces, in murals, and even as an exterior cladding in warmer climates. Mosaic tiles are units less than 6 square inches and are available glazed or unglazed. They are usually mounted at the factory onto sheets of paper about 2 feet square. The individual tiles are spaced to allow a cement grout to be placed between them. Quarry tile is an unglazed clay or shale floor tile that is very durable and impervious to moisture. Clay pavers are also unglazed, resembling mosaic tile, though having an area of more than 6 square inches.

The wide variety of sizes permits combinations of tiles to be used in the same layout.

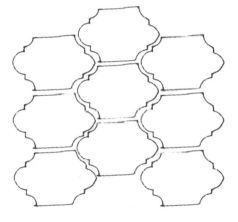

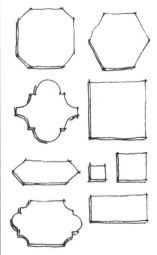

Numerous colorful and textured patterns can be made from different tile shapes.

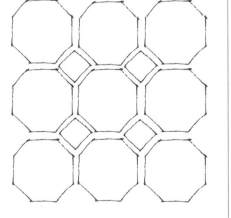

THE TILES OF SANTA CATALINA ISLAND

This salvaged tile from a Catalina building was reused in a simple planter base.

Santa Catalina Island, just twenty miles offshore from Los Angeles, California, is an oasis of tile work. This eccentric island, well known for its ties to the Wrigley family of chewing gum fame, has an interesting history with ceramics. In the early 1920s, William Wrigley and David Renton developed a brick and tile factory, prompted by the discovery of clay deposits. Mr. Wrigley felt that manufacturing building materials on the island would reduce the cost of many of his planned building projects. Catalina Clay Products focused on manufacturing materials such as bricks and roofing tile during the first few years in operation. In the 1930s, the company expanded its line to include decorative ware and tiles. The tile plant included artists' studios, research laboratories, molding rooms, kilns, assembly rooms, a glazing room, and a storage yard. Catalina Clay Products manufactured tile only until 1937, but the rich architecture on the island continues the colorful, unique ceramic heritage. Today, evidence of Wrigley and Renton's discovery is visible throughout Santa Catalina Island.

This bus stop bench incorporates colorful glazed tiles for the backrest, and large clay tiles for the seat.

A variety of tile designs were used to create this interesting public fountain.

The tile border on this planter creates a strong, colorful contrast with the white plaster base.

REUSE

Boxes of surplus tile. Many decorative tile renovations can be done with surplus tiles or discontinued stock. If you have some broken tiles, or are missing tiles on your entry floor or in your shower stall, buy some contrasting color tiles to add a fun pattern while filling in the missing pieces. (You may have to remove a few more existing tiles for the new pattern to become repetitive). You can buy discontinued tiles at used building material stores for approximately one-quarter the price of new tile, but you won't find a large volume of any certain color or style. The only tools that you will require to take on a tile renovation are a measuring tape, a notched trowel to evenly spread ceramic adhesive, some grout to match what has already been used, and a couple of sponges to wipe the tiles after they have been grouted. Try making a pattern to look like a small floor mat in your entry or bathroom. The Italians are famous for their ceramic floor designs representing Persian carpets.

Surprisingly, ceramics may be one of the most important and valuable materials to consider reusing in your home renovation. Due to the cost of fossil fuels to fire the product, it is beneficial to keep that investment in use. Although relatively inert as a landfill material, ceramics can take up valuable space, and take virtually forever to decompose. California's water restriction policies have deemed that many toilet fixtures consume too much water, and more water-efficient low-flow units are recommended. This surplus of regular toilets presents valuable reuse opportunties. Many of these toilets can be adapted with tank dams or low-flow adaptors to increase their water efficiency.

One of the difficulties inherent in working with salvaged ceramics is that thousands of different styles and colors are available in everything from toilets, sinks, and tubs, to floor, counter, and wainscoting tiles. Trying to match or replace a broken component can be frustrating. Each manufacturer changes colors and patterns annually to keep competitive. In addition, varying clay bodies can affect final product size after firing. Although the modern tile industry has adopted sizing standards, older pieces may not be consistently sized. Still, many resourceful renovators will find that reusing ceramic pieces poses a challenging puzzle, rather than an annoying problem.

SAFETY ALERT

Always wear safety glasses when cutting or breaking ceramic tiles. The edges are as sharp as glass, and the brittle material can fracture into knifelike shards. To be safe, handle broken ceramics with work gloves at all times.

FROM TILE TO TILE

Reclaimed tiles can often be found at architectural salvage or used building material stores. Small batches of ceramic tiles might not be enough to cover a whole floor, but they can be incorporated into large-scale designs or used to create a fireplace or a sink border. Tile manufacturers often offer great discounts on discontinued, out-of-date, or damaged stock. Ask to see what might not be on the display racks. Cracked or incomplete tiles are useful too, if you want to make a mosaic tile piece.

Sunburst tile design in a mosaic field. Ceramic tile artist Sherry Schalm has used a variety of tiles to make this attractive entry foyer floor design. It may be more time consuming than laying linoleum, but the effect will be much more dramatic. Sherry first drew a full-scale design on paper, to calculate the quantity and sizes of tiles required for the pattern. Then she simply shaped the tiles using tile cutters, and laid down the pieces on the paper pattern prior to cementing each tile piece to the floor.

Pottery shards for mosaic work. I found these ceramic fragments at the oceanside in rural Nova Scotia. They were likely discarded broken dishes thrown in a rubbish heap over a century ago. Mosaics used in decorative works need not be completely flat and smooth on top.

TILE TABLE

This table is a great example of how tiles can be reused. Mosaics are also a fun way to make a table surface, though this utilization of four large tiles is much easier and less time consuming to build. Similar to the plank table and the cast grate table seen in earlier chapters, this table utilizes what many are so quick to throw away. Almost every tiling job in the home results in leftover whole or cut-off pieces. This table uses salvaged wooden spindles for legs, wood molding and plywood for the base of the tabletop, and four 12-by-12-inch ceramic tiles for the top. Construct the base for the table, including the molding edge on the plywood. Plan for the tile and adhesive thickness to be flush with the top of the molding. Building the top is similar to laying tile on the floor or wall. Use a notched trowel and ceramic adhesive to make a proper mortar bed for the tile on the plywood top. Work tile grout into the seams between the tiles and the molding to fill in the spaces between the tiles.

KIDS' TILE PROJECTS

This is a perfect use for leftover and broken tiles. Your kids can create fun, usable objects with different colored and shaped tiles. Most kids already have the things they need for this project: white glue, felt, scissors, heavy colored cardboard or boxboard, and markers or colored pencils.

Ahead of time, break the tiles with a hammer on a concrete surface (wearing safety goggles). The tiles should be approximately two inches square for mosaic work.

Coasters are a good project for kids from ages five to seven. They can glue all shapes and sizes of ceramic tile to a piece of felt to create a coaster. Kids can also draw or glue shapes on the whole tiles.

For kids aged eight to ten, trivets (hot plates) or tile mosaics are great projects. For a trivet, prepare pieces of ½-inch plywood, approximately 8 inches square. In a vise, attach 1-inch wood molding to the edge of the plywood, using a mitred corner. Nail the molding so that the the finished tile will be level with the molding.

Kids can make their own mosaic art, using ceramic adhesive to attach various pieces of tile to a piece of plywood. With a notched trowel, cover the working area with ceramic adhesive. For both trivets and

mosaics, it is best if the tile pieces are laid tight to each other with only a small amount of grout to fill in the gaps once the glue has dried. Push grout into the cracks between the tile pieces with a flexible putty knife. Wipe excess grout off the tiles with damp sponge and let the pieces dry.

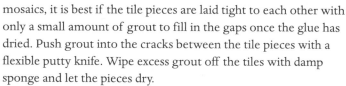

THE UTILITY OF CERAMIC FIXTURES

Salvaged porcelain light fixture. Porcelain and glass have been used for decades as electrical insulators. Porcelains are classified into two types: low-voltage and high-voltage. Low-voltage porcelain is generally used to insulate 110-volt AC applications. High-voltage porcelain is vitrified and can withstand all higher voltages and extreme temperatures. The ceramic products used in electronics can vary from electrical line insulators for wiring, spark plug insulation, and cables and casings for electronics.

Wall of salvaged sinks.
Ceramic plumbing fixtures are made from glazed, vitreous clays. Early plumbing fixtures were made from a more porous clay, though today's vitreous clay is much superior in performance. The added difficulty in firing and drying large ceramic bodies, such as toilets and sinks, is that it is a precise art to avoid cracking of the finish and still provide an impervious, continuous surface.

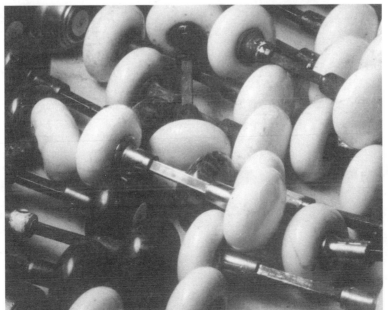

Various colored porcelain doorknobs. Some of the simplest and most functional hardware is made from ceramic. During the late 1800s, porcelain was widely used for doorknobs, collars, escutcheons, light fixtures, cabinet pulls, light switch cores, and decorative elements. Some porcelain fixtures may still be found, though most have been replaced by metal, glass, or plastic. Porcelain hardware is still popular in bathrooms, as much of it is designed to be incorporated with ceramic wall tile. The impervious nature of ceramic hardware makes it perfect for use in bathrooms and kitchens. Toilet paper dispensers, toothbrush holders, and towel bars and rings are bathroom accessories often made of ceramic.

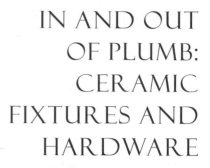

IN AND OUT OF PLUMB: CERAMIC FIXTURES AND HARDWARE

GARDENING SINK

My neighbor Susan uses a salvaged porcelain laundry sink for her gardening work. This old, chipped, and rusted porcelain sink would be too costly to refurbish for use in the home, but with a garden hose to supply water and a bucket below, it makes an affordable outdoor utility sink. Unlike their predecessors, most new sinks don't have heavy, solid cast bases, which perform well in outdoor climes and in heavy use areas. Susan built the table to support the sink from scrap 2 x 4s and a piece of plywood for a storage shelf, and mounted wood screws and salvaged coat hooks on the front for conviently hanging gardening handtools. She bought this sink at a used building material store for $10.

Plumbing fixtures, out of context as plant base. Some ceramic objects just can't be reused efficiently in their original applications. The tank for this toilet has been out of production for a long time, and would be difficult to reconfigure. The detailing on this Victorian porcelain toilet base makes it a perfect planter and conversation piece.

Toilets and sinks in a variety of colors. Most used building material stores have plumbing fixtures available in a rainbow of colors, featuring the broad array of hues that have been trendy during one period or another. Wall-hung sinks are usually the most affordable, costing only $25 (CAD) for the sink and taps, whereas some of the old antique porcelain pedestal sinks can cost in the range of $250 to $600 (CAD). When buying old fixtures, ensure that the bowl of a sink or bathtub has an overflow opening. Many building codes will not permit fixtures without an overflow, due to the danger of flooding that would cause building damage.

A before-and-after renovated bathroom using salvaged fixtures and a painted plywood floor. One of the easiest ways to renovate a bathroom on a budget is to utilize used plumbing fixtures. This idea doesn't appeal to many people, but if you consider that a toilet is only new until the first flush, you might change your mind. Plumbing fixtures removed from commercial and institutional buildings often exceed the quality required for most residential applications. Many toilets have been replaced due to water restrictions in their region, though, depending on the water-consumption rate allowed, many older toilets can be fitted with low-flow adaptors to continue their use.

Refinished tub in a refurbished farmhouse. If the porcelain finish appears or feels worn, a reglazing process can brighten up the inside of the tub. You can upgrade the outside surface of the tub by simply wire brushing off any accumulated rust or debris. Use any color of metal paint to finish the outer surface. Some homeowners choose to paint the decorative feet, while others take the extra effort to wire brush them to their original cast-iron finish.

Salvaged ball and claw tubs. Old ball and claw bathtubs provide some of the best examples of reuse. These porcelain-finished tubs have a cast-iron base that will hold heat better than any steel or fiberglass model on the market today. The hardware for these tubs is fairly standard and can easily be purchased at a plumbing supply store.

THE $62 BATHROOM

Simple ceramic pieces . . . Sometimes in a renovation, the bottom dollar doesn't need to mean skimping on quality. In my own home, a century-old farmhouse now in a city neighborhood, I needed a half-bath on the main floor. Though little area was available for the bathroom, the budget was even smaller than the allowable space. The main requirements were a toilet, sink, mirror, and light fixture. I found all of these items at a used building material store for $62 (U.S.).

. . . for an affordable half-bath. Every fixture in the bathroom was salvaged, including the towel bar and glass shelf. The mirror comes from an old cabinet door. You can see the salvaged porcelain light fixture on page 147. The room is efficient, simple, and provides exactly the use that was intended.

Toilet	$25 U.S.
Sink	15
Mirror	5
Light fixture	10
Glass shelf	5
Toilet paper holder	1
Towel bar	1
TOTAL	$62

RECYCLING

At present little is being done with ceramic building materials in the recycling industry. Ceramics can be crushed and used as a roadbase aggregate with qualities similar to that of brick, except for the ceramic surface glazing. Each color of glazing contains a different chemical element, which would be costly to remove during the recycling process.

Still, crushed ceramic is not considered a dangerous material as landfill, and is used as "clean fill" in many regions. Crushed ceramics are useful in areas of difficult drainage, as the slick surface of most glazes transfers water with ease.

FACT

When the inventor Joseph Bramah, a Yorkshireman, was asked to refit a new water closet, he was disappointed by its poor design. Thus Bramah patented the flush toilet in 1778. Bramahís design included a hinged valve, instead of a sliding valve, under the pan, and a handle, which opened the valve to let out the contents. A delay mechanism kept the water running for fifteen seconds to refill the pan.

Contrary to the popular belief that he invented the toilet, Thomas Crapper merely improved upon the syphonic flush system. His company, Thos. Crapper & Co., was started in 1861 and survived until 1966.

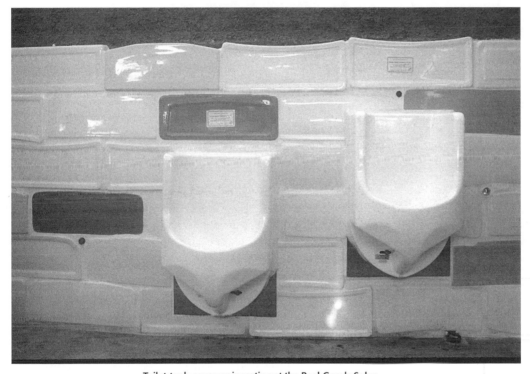

Toilet-tank-cover wainscoting at the Real Goods Solar Living Center, Hopland, California. Some jurisdictions in California, where water conservation is the utmost concern, legislate that all new installed toilets must meet minimum consumption requirements (1.3 Imperial gallons/1.6 U.S. gallons/6 liters per flush). As a result, Californians are landfilling many older, larger volume toilets. Some have made efforts to retrofit the toilets with low-flow devices, or to ship the toilets to regions where water conservation measures are not so stringent.

THE $1,000 KITCHEN

An island of salvaged materials and appliances. Nadine designed this island to be the main preparation and cooking area. She wanted to create a centerpiece where people could congregate and participate in the cooking. The island countertop was made from salvaged pine boards and trim, with several coats of a water-based finish. A second plank, hinged to the island, folds down to create extra room for standing when many people congregate in what has become the most popular room in the house. The owners use the folding counter for quick morning meals. The other countertop is a modern-style laminate on a particleboard base. Short lengths of this type of countertop can often be purchased from used building material stores, or as end-of-stock at a discount from the manufacturer. The wall oven built into the base of the island, the cooktop above, and the refrigerator were purchased secondhand for $400.

The renovation of this kitchen was an adventure for its owners, Robert and Nadine, a young couple with lots of energy and a very restricted budget. The challenge was not only to accomplish the goal of completely furnishing the kitchen on a tight budget, but to respect the age of the building and not put in a modern-looking design. The home was built in 1896 and has softwood plank flooring throughout and beaded wooden wainscoting in the kitchen.

The room, only 10 by 12 feet, was not the original kitchen prior to this renovation. The century-old house had a tiny pantry-kitchen in a small addition to the rear of the house—too small for the owners to work side-by-side. Even the placement of the essential appliances was difficult, as two windows and four doors led into the small room. The owners replaced one door with a window frame matching the style of the others in the house. They maintained and painted the wainscoting.

The cost for the materials for this renovation, including appliances, was $1,123

Reused upper cabinets	$10 (CAD)
Salvaged base cabinets	240
Salvaged sink	150
Salvaged countertop	72
Salvaged island countertop	36
Secondhand cooktop & oven	150
Secondhand refrigerator	250
Salvaged fluorescent light fixture	5
New halogen light fixtures	160
Paint, caulk, and other materials	50
	$1,123 (CAD)

Reused cupboards and salvaged cabinets. The upper cupboards were salvaged from the original pantry-kitchen. The unit was site-built and required little modification to be reused. The glass doors provide a pleasing effect and the open shelves are convenient for frequently used dishes. The very high-quality base cabinets came from a used building material store. Only one coat of paint was required to spruce them up.

(CAD). The owners enjoyed the process of trying to meet their budget. They worked evenings and weekends to accomplish this kitchen renovation in less than two weeks, and only hired a plumber and electrician to do the final connections. Robert feels that they could have met their budget, had it not been for the last-minute decision to purchase two brand new halogen light fixtures. Salvaging materials almost always saves money.

Kitchen walls stripped of broken plaster, with wainscoting still in place. Old plaster can lose its strength if the keys of the plaster pushed in between the wood laths break or deteriorate. It was necessary to strip the plaster walls above the original wainscoting.

Kitchen walls with new sheetrock and paint.

The porcelain sink with drainboard was salvaged from a maternity hospital, and is the focus of a lot of activity in this kitchen without a dishwasher. The sink sits on salvaged cabinetry upon the original softwood plank floor.

RESOURCES

American Institute of Architects
(AIA)
Committee on the Environment
1735 New York Avenue, NW
Washington, D.C. 20006
(202) 626-7463
www.aiaonline.com/

Canada Mortgage and Housing
Corporation (CMHC)
682 Montreal Road
Ottawa, Ontario
Canada K1A 0P7
(613) 748-2000
www.cmhc-schl.gc.ca

Center for Renewable and
Environmentally Sustainable
Technologies (CREST)
1612 K Street NW, Suite 410
Washington, DC 20006
http://soltice.crest.org/

Center for Resourceful Building
Technology (CRBT)
P.O. Box 100
Missoula, MT 59806
(406) 549-7678
www.montana.com/crbt/
mis.html

Energy Efficient Building
Association (EEBA)
10740 Lyndale Avenue South
Bloomington, MN 55420-5615
(952) 881-1098
www.eeba.org

Environment Canada
123 Main Street, Suite 150
Winnipeg, Manitoba
Canada R3C 4W2
www.ec.gc.ca

Environmental Building News (EBN)
122 Birge Street, Suite 30
Brattleboro, VT 05301
(802) 257-7300
www.buildinggreen.com

Environmental Construction
Outfitters
44 Crosby Street
New York, NY 10012
(212) 334-9659 or (800) 238-5008

Environmental Protection Agency
(EPA)
www.smartgrowth.org (look
under Smart Buildings,
Deconstruction Resources)

Green Building Information
Council (GBIC)
http://greenbuilding.ca

Halifax County Construction and
Debris Recycling Limited
(HCCDRL)
16 Mills Drive
Goodwood, Nova Scotia
Canada B3T 1P3
(902) 876-8644

National Association of Home
Builders Research Center
(NAHB)
400 Prince George's Boulevard
Upper Marlboro, MD 20774-8731
(301) 249-4000
www.nahbrc.org

Oakdene Community Centre
Bear River, Nova Scotia, Canada
Project Manager, Robbie Bays
(902) 467-3939
E-mail: oakdene@glinx.com

Recycler's World
P.O. Box 1910
Richfield Springs, NY 13439
www.recycle.net

Renovators Resource Inc.
P.O. Box 36032
Halifax, Nova Scotia
Canada B3J 3S9
(902) 429-3889
www.renovators-resource.com

Reuse Development Organization
(ReDO)
P.O. Box 441363
Indianapolis, IN 46244
(317) 631-5395
www.redo.org

Resource Renewal Institute
www.rri.org/

ReUse Centre
2216 East Last Street
Minneapolis, MN 55407
(612) 724-2608
www.greeninstitute.org

Salvo Web
Ford Village
Berwick-upon-Tweed
TD15 2QG
Northumberland, England
441-890-820-333
http://salvo.co.uk

Used Building Material Association
(UBMA)
P.O. Box 196, 1096 Queen Street
Halifax, Nova Scotia
Canada B3H 2R9
toll-free: 1 (877) 221-8262
www.ubma.org

BIBLIOGRAPHY

Blandford, Percy W. *Practical Blacksmithing and Metalworking.* New York: TAB Books, 1988.

Byrne, Michael. *Setting Tile.* Newtown, Conn.: Taunton Press, 1995.

Byrne, Richard O. "Conservation of Historic Window Glass." APT Bulletin 13, no. 3 (1981).

Curtis, John Obed. "Moving Historic Buildings." U.S. Dept. of the Interior, Heritage Conservation and Recreation Service, Technical Preservation Services Division, 1979.

Crossland, John R., and J. M. Parrish. *The Treasury of Modern Marvels.* London: Collins Clear Type Press, 1937.

Decker, Phillip J., and T. Newell Decker. *Renovating Brick Houses.* Pownal, Vt.: Garden Way Publishing, 1990.

Gascoigne, R. M. "Construction & Demolition Waste Management with References to Embodied Energy and Life Cycle Costs." Thesis, Somerset University, School of Management, December 1995.

Geerlings, Gerald K. *Wrought Iron in Architecture: Wrought Iron Craftsmanship.* New York: C. Scribner's & Sons, 1929.

Gloag, John, and Derek Bridgwater. *A History of Cast Iron in Architecture.* New York: G. Allen and Unwin, 1948.

Hart-Davis, Adam. *Thunder, Flush and Thomas Crapper: An Encyclopedia.* London: Trafalger Square, 1997.

Home Decorating Institute. *Decorating with Great Finds—82 Ways to Use Finds from Antique Stores, Garage Sales & Attics.* Minneapolis: Cy Decosse Incorporated, 1995.

Hornbostel, Caleb. *Construction Materials, Types, Uses and Applications.* New York: John Wiley & Sons, 1978.

Hoyle, Fred. *On Stonehenge.* San Francisco: W. H. Freeman and Company, 1977.

Hutchins, Nigel. *Restoring Old Houses.* Toronto: Van Nostrand Reinhold, 1982.

Jenkins, Joseph. *The Slate Roof Bible.* Grove City, Penn.: Jenkins Publishing, 1997.

Lee, P. William. *Ceramics.* New York: Reinhold Publishing, 1961.

Litchfield, Michael, and Rosmarie Hausher. *Salvaged Treasures.* New York: Van Nostrand Reinhold, 1983.

Long, Charles. *The Stonebuilder's Primer.* Willowdale, Ontario: Firefly Books, 1998.

Maddex, Diane. *All About Old Buildings.* National Trust for Historic Preservation. Washington, D.C.: The Preservation Press, 1985.

Masonry. The Best of Fine Homebuilding series. Newtown, Conn.: Taunton, 1997.

McKee, Harley J. *Introduction to Early American Masonry, Stone, Brick, Mortar and Plaster.* Washington, D.C.: National Trust/Columbia University Series on the Technology of Early American Building, 1973.

McRaven, Charles. *Building with Stone.* Pownal, Vt.: Storey, 1989.

Merit Students Encyclopedia, vol. 13, Wiliam D. Halsey, ed. New York: Cromwell-Collier Education Corp. 1971.

Mumma, Tracy. *Guide to Resource Efficient Building Elements.* 6th ed. Missoula: Center for Resourceful Building Technology, 1997.

Pearson, David. *The Natural House Book.* New York: Simon & Schuster, 1989.

Peterson, Charles E. *Building Early America: Proceedings of the Symposium Held at Philadelphia to Celebrate the 250th Birthday of the Carpenters Company of the City and County of Philadelphia.* Radnor, Pennsylvania: Chilton Book Company, 1976.

Rendle, B. J. *Fifty Years of Timber Research: A Short History of the Forest Products Research Laboratory.* Baltimore: Princes Risborough, 1976.

Robertson, E. Graeme. *Cast Iron Decoration: A World Survey*. London: Thames & Hudson, 1977.

Rodriguez, Mario. *Traditional Woodwork: Adding Authentic Period Details to Any Home*. Newtown, Conn.: Taunton Press, 1998.

Rosenhain, Walter. *Glass Manufacture*. 2nd ed. London: Constable Press, 1919.

Roy, Rob. *The Sauna*. White River Junction, Vt.: Chelsea Green Publishing, 1996.

Roy, Rob. *Stone Circles: A Modern Builder's Guide to the Megalithic Revival*. White River Junction, Vt.: Chelsea Green Publishing, 1996.

Schaeffer, John. *A Place in the Sun: The Evolution of the Real Goods Solar Living Center*. White River Junction, Vt.: Chelsea Green Publishing, 1997.

Smith, R.C. *Material of Construction*. 3rd ed. New York, McGraw-Hill, 1979.

Vesilind, Priit J. "In Search of Vikings." *National Geographic* 197, no. 5 (May 2000): 27.

Wing, Daniel, and Alan Scott. *The Bread Builders: Hearth Loaves and Masonry Ovens*. White River Junction, Vt.: Chelsea Green Publishing, 1999.

PHOTOGRAPHY CREDITS

Robbie Bays (132, 133); Kelly Bentham (26, 27, 28 [nailed and plugged screw connections], 29, 30 [bedframe, chest of drawers, drawer pulls], 31 [door headboard], 32 [shutters, shutter shelf], 33, 34, 35, 39, 40, 41, 42, 44 [cast iron bathtub feet], 45, 46, 47, 50 [cast iron grates], 55, 56 [security grill, metal grill, wall sconce], 57 [hospital cabinetry], 59 [copper humidifier, wine rack], 60, 61 [light restoration specialist, copper light fixture], 66 [stone tile finishes], 68, 71, 73 [stone parapet], 81, 85 [slate mantel], 87, 90, 91, 94 [clay pipe], 96, 97, 103, 104, 105 cleaning brick], 106, 114 [sand], 115 [assortment of glass], 120 [thermopane windows], 121 [modern stained-glass], 123 [mirror, glass blocks], 124 [salvaged windows], 125 [after], 126 [multi-pane heat register], 127, 130, 137 [variety of tiles], 144, 146 [tile table], 147 [porcelain doorknobs], 148 [toilet planter, toilets and sinks], 149 [before and after], 152, 153 [cupboards and cabinets); Lorin Brehaut (22, 23); R. Button (73 [stone house]); Rachael Cohen (149, refinished tub); Jennifer Corson (xi, xii, xiii, 1, 15 [milled 2 x 6s, transport truck], 16, 25, 26, 30 [salvaged door], 31 [door bench], 49 [blacksmith, hinge], 51, 54, 57 [cast iron grate table], 67, 73, 76, 77, 78, 79 [granite steps], 80 [basalt pavers], 82, 86, 88, 89, 93, 94 [stacked adobe], 99, 105 [brick pile], 110 [brick chips], 121 [church window], 124 [discontinued windows], 125 [before, salvaged thermopane], 129, 131, 134, 135, 138, 139, 145 [pottery shards], 146 [tile trivet], 147 [salvaged light fixture, wall of sinks], 149 [salvaged tubs], 150, 153 [porcelain sink, stripped walls, restored walls]); courtesy of Faculty of Architecture, Daltech University (53 [John Hancock Center], 114 [sky-scraper], 123 [curtain wall system]); Richard Freeman (102, masonry bread oven); Arwed Gerstenberger, courtesy of Nova Tile and Marble Ltd. (66 [marble quarry face], 70 [quarrying landscape pavers], 75); Michael Gorman (117); Susan Helliwell (58 [faucet coat rack], 67, 81); Emmanuel Jannesch (20, 126 [office renovation]); Joe Jenkins (84); Michael MacDonald (69); Harold Mills (95, 107 [brick path]); Joan Mortimer (109, brick barbecue); courtesy of NAHB Research Center (64, 65); courtesy of Nova Scotia Department of Natural Resources (10, 11, 12, 14, 18, 19, 48, 70 [quarry operation], 98, 99, 100, 103 [high-rise]); Jeff Oldham (151); courtesy of Pittsburgh Plate Glass Canada Ltd. (120, float glass factory); courtesy of Pick & Shovel Productions Ltd. 15 [mill pond, sawmill operator], 21, 24 [garden gate], 32 [pot rack], 36, 37, 38, 53 [nails and screws], 56 [bathtub leg and cast], 58 [doorknob coat rack, knob close-up], 59 [rebar door handle], 61 [light restorer's inventory], 79 [bench], 83, 102 [beehive oven], 103 [masonry heater], 128, 148 [garden sink]); courtesy of Gordon Pinsent and Independent Pictures Inc. (21); courtesy of G. R. Plume Company (24, salvaged timber); Chris Reardon (28 [salvaged flooring], 126, 140, 145 [mosaic floor]); courtesy of Renovators Resource Ltd. (57, 108 [open-hearth fireplace], 147); Keith Robertson (49 [armillary sphere], 50 [skyscraper], 53, 72, 82, 101, 125, 149); courtesy of J. Ross and Sons Ltd. (62); Rob Roy (69, 79 [standing stones], 85 [slate floor]); Norbert Senf (107 [brick floor], 108 [woodstove base]); courtesy of Tangerine Tileworks (142, 143); Martha Twombly (80 [fieldstone patio], 109 [brick fireback]); Joyce Wisdom (111, 112, 113).

CHELSEA GREEN

Sustainable living has many facets. Chelsea Green's celebration of the sustainable arts has led us to publish trend-setting books about organic gardening, solar electricity and renewable energy, innovative building techniques, regenerative forestry, local and bioregional democracy, and whole foods. The company's published works, while intensely practical, are also entertaining and inspirational, demonstrating that an ecological approach to life is consistent with producing beautiful, eloquent, and useful books, videos, and audio cassettes.

For more information about Chelsea Green, or to request a free catalog, call toll-free (800) 639–4099, or write to us at P.O. Box 428, White River Junction, Vermont 05001. Visit our Web site at www.chelseagreen.com.

Chelsea Green's titles include:

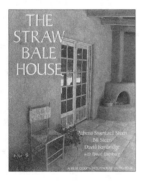

The Straw Bale House
The New Independent Home
Independent Builder:
  Designing & Building a House
  Your Own Way
The Rammed Earth House
The Passive Solar House
The Earth-Sheltered House
Wind Energy Basics
The Solar Living Sourcebook
Mortgage-Free!
The Beauty of Straw
 Bale Homes
The Natural House
Serious Straw Bale:
  A Home Construction Guide
  for All Climates

Four-Season Harvest
The Apple Grower
The Flower Farmer
Passport to Gardening
The New Organic Grower
Solar Gardening
Straight-Ahead Organic
Good Spirits
The Contrary Farmer
The Contrary Farmer's
  Invitation to Gardening
Whole Foods Companion
The Bread Builders
The Co-op Cookbook
Keeping Food Fresh
The Neighborhood Forager
Simple Food for the Good Life

Believing Cassandra
Gaviotas: A Village to Reinvent
  the World
Beyond the Limits
The Man Who Planted Trees
Who Owns the Sun?
Global Spin: The Corporate
  Assault on Environmentalism
Seeing Nature
Hemp Horizons
Genetic Engineering, Food, and
  Our Environment
Scott Nearing: The Making
  of a Home Steader
Loving and Leaving the
  Good Life
Wise Words for the Good Life